# Excel 4 for Windows™ Quick Reference

**Que Quick Reference Series**

DON ROCHE, JR.

# CREDITS

**Publisher**
Lloyd J. Short

**Acquisitions Editor**
Tim Ryan

**Production Editor**
Cindy Morrow

**Editors**
Barbara Koenig
Pamela Wampler
Laura Wirthlin

**Technical Editor**
Lynda A. Fox

**Production Team**
Claudia Bell
Brook Farling
Audra Hershman
Betty Kish
Bob LaRoche
Laurie Lee
Juli Pavey
Caroline Roop
Susan VandeWalle
Mary Beth Wakefield
Phil Worthington

# TRADEMARK ACKNOWLEDGMENTS

1-2-3 and Lotus are registered trademarks of Lotus Development Corporation.

Microsoft, Microsoft Excel, and Microsoft Windows are registered trademarks of Microsoft Corporation.

# TABLE OF CONTENTS

v

# INTRODUCTION

*Excel 4 for Windows Quick Reference* is not a rehash of the Excel 4 for Windows documentation. Rather, the book is a compilation of readily available, hands-on material that will enable you to use Excel 4 for Windows more confidently.

This handy guide is a perfect book to sit next to your computer and serve as a reference when you have questions about Excel procedures and methods. The book is a natural for both beginning users and Excel veterans.

The book is divided into two sections. The first, an Excel Overview, explains the basics of Excel and the new features added to Excel 4 for Windows. The second section, Command Reference, leads you step-by-step through each Excel command. The commands are listed in alphabetical order so that you can instantly find the information you need.

If you are new to Excel and would like a complete overview of the program's capabilities, pick up a copy of Que's *Using Excel 4 for Windows,* Special Edition.

# AN EXCEL OVERVIEW

You can use Microsoft Excel to perform calculations, analyze data, access external databases, chart data and create graphics, perform "what-if" analyses, outline worksheets, consolidate worksheets, customize formats, and automate routine tasks with macros.

You access Excel's power through menus, command lists, Toolbars, and "quick-key" keystrokes.

## Choosing Menu Items

The *menu bar*, the second line in the worksheet window, shows the menu selections. You can choose a menu item using the keyboard or the mouse.

### *To choose a menu item using the keyboard*

1. Press **Alt** to activate the menu bar.

2. Press the underlined letter in the menu you want to see. (It does not matter whether you type the letter in upper- or lowercase.) In this book, the keys you press appear in blue and boldface type.

3. Press the underlined letter of the command you want to use.

   Commands that are not available for selection appear dimmed.

### To choose a menu item using the mouse

1. Move the mouse pointer to the menu you want.

2. Click the mouse button to see the menu.

3. Move the pointer to the command you want.

   Commands that are not available for selection appear dimmed.

4. Click the command to select it.

If the command name is followed by an ellipsis (...), a dialog box appears prompting you for more information.

## Using Shortcut Menus

The shortcut menu provides a quick way to make a spreadsheet change. Click both the left and right mouse buttons at the same time. A menu of choices appears on-screen. The choices depend on the state of the worksheet or whether you are in a worksheet, macro sheet, or chart.

# Accessing Dialog Boxes

Dialog boxes can consist of the following elements:

- A *list box* is a rectangular area that displays a list of choices.

- A *text box* is a rectangular area where you can enter relevant text or numbers.

- A *check box* is a small square box used to turn on or off a particular option.

- An *option button* is a small round button used to turn on one of a group of options.

- A *command button* is a rounded rectangular button labeled with a particular action.

- A *drop-down list* is a small rectangular area that displays one item in a list and has a down arrow to the right of the item that you use to display the complete list of choices.

Using the keyboard, you can move around a dialog box by pressing Tab to go forward and Shift+Tab to go backward. To select a dialog box option, press Alt and the underlined letter or number for the option.

Using the mouse, move the pointer to the option and click. You can use ↑ and ↓ to move up and down, respectively, through an active list box. You also can use the PgUp and PgDn keys for this function. To locate a specific item, simply press the initial letter key for that item; you will move directly to the first item in the list beginning with that letter. If necessary, you then can press ↓ or the PgDn key to move to the item.

You also can move up and down through a list in an active list box by clicking the scroll bars. When the item you need appears, move the mouse pointer to the item and click.

Pressing the space bar turns an active check box on or off. Clicking the check box also turns the choice on or off.

Pressing Enter selects OK, unless the active command button has been moved to a different choice. You can also click the OK command button. Pressing Enter is usually the fastest way to accept the dialog box settings, close the dialog box, and execute the command. Pressing Esc always selects the Cancel command button, which usually cancels any changes to your dialog settings and then closes the dialog box.

## Navigating

To move to a cell using the mouse, move the pointer to the cell you want to select and then click. If the cell is not on-screen, first use the scroll bars to locate and display the cell. If the cell is not in the current window but can be seen on-screen, move the mouse pointer to the cell you want to select and click. If the cell is not in the current window and cannot be seen on-screen, select the window from under the Window menu, locate the cell, and click.

Use the Num Lock key to toggle between pointer-movement keys and number-key entries.

To move to a cell using the keyboard, use the following key(s). A plus sign (+) indicates that you must hold down the first key, press the second key, and then release both keys.

| Key(s) | Function |
|--------|----------|
| ← | Moves active cell left one cell. |
| → | Moves active cell right one cell. |
| ↑ | Moves active cell up one cell. |
| ↓ | Moves active cell down one cell. |

| Key(s) | Function |
| --- | --- |
| Home | Moves active cell to the beginning of the current row. |
| End+→ | Unless Scroll Lock is on, moves the active cell right to the next intersection of a blank cell and a cell that contains data in the current row. |
| End+← | Unless Scroll Lock is on, moves the active cell left to the next intersection of a blank cell and a cell that contains data in the current row. |
| End+↑ | Unless Scroll Lock is on, moves the active cell up to the next intersection of a blank cell and a cell that contains data in the current column. |
| End+↓ | Unless Scroll Lock is on, moves the active cell down to the next intersection of a blank cell and a cell that contains data in the current column. |
| End+Home | Unless Scroll Lock is on, moves the active cell to the last active cell of the current worksheet. |
| Home | If Scroll Lock is on, moves the active cell to the upper left corner of the window. |
| End | If Scroll Lock is on, moves the active cell to the lower right corner of the window. |
| PgUp | Moves the active cell up one screen. |
| PgDn | Moves the active cell down one screen. |
| Ctrl+PgUp | Moves the active cell left one screen. |
| Ctrl+PgDn | Moves the active cell right one screen. |
| Ctrl+Home | Moves the active cell to cell A1 of the current worksheet. |

| Key(s) | Function |
|--------|----------|
| Ctrl+End | Moves the active cell to the last active cell of the current worksheet. |
| Ctrl+← | Moves the active cell left to the next intersection of a blank cell and a cell that contains data in the current row. |
| Ctrl+→ | Moves the active cell right to the next intersection of a blank cell and a cell that contains data in the current row. |
| Ctrl+↑ | Moves the active cell up to the next intersection of a blank cell and a cell that contains data in the current column. |
| Ctrl+↓ | Moves the active cell down to the next intersection of a blank cell and a cell that contains data in the current column. |
| F5 (GoTo) | Prompts for a cell reference, range, or range name. After you select or enter the information and press Enter, activates that reference. |
| Alt, W, window# | Moves the active cell from the current (active) window to another window whose number you specify. |

## Selecting

Some commands require that you select a cell, range, multiple areas, chart object, or another item. The following chart explains selection methods.

| To select... | Do this... |
|--------------|------------|
| An item with the mouse | Click that item. |

| To select... | Do this... |
| --- | --- |
| Adjacent items | Click the first item and drag to highlight the other items. |
| Nonadjacent items | Press down the Ctrl key while selecting each item after the first. |
| A row | Click the row number. |
| Multiple rows | Click a row number and drag up or down. |
| A column | Click the column letter. |
| Multiple columns | Click a column letter and drag left or right. Click the gray rectangle directly above row 1 and directly to the left of column A to select the entire worksheet. |

To unselect something, click anywhere on the worksheet.

To select items with the keyboard, use these keys:

| Key(s) | Function |
| --- | --- |
| Shift+ | Selects as you move. Combine Shift with any of the movement keys listed in the preceding section. For instance, Shift+Home extends the selection to the beginning for the row. |
| Shift+space bar | Selects an entire row. |
| Ctrl+space bar | Selects an entire column. |
| Ctrl+* | Selects the current data block. |
| Shift+Ctrl+ space bar | Selects the entire worksheet. |

| Key(s) | Function |
|---|---|
| F8 (Extend) | Extends the selection as you move (as if you were pressing Shift) and anchors the corner cell of the selection. To end Extend mode, press F8 again. |
| Shift+F8 (Add) | Puts Excel in Add mode, adding to the current selection another area that is not adjacent to the current selection. To end Add mode, press Shift+F8 again. |
| F5 (GoTo) | Prompts for a cell reference, range, or range name. If you enter a range or a range name and press Enter, the range is selected. |
| F8, F5 | Extends a selection from the current (active) cell to the cell you move to using F5. |
| F5, Shift+Enter | Extends a selection from the current (active) cell to the cell you move to using F5. After pressing F5 and entering the cell address, press down the Shift key and press Enter. |

# Moving Within a Selection

Using the cursor-movement keys within a selection unselects it. To move within a selection, use the following keys:

| Key(s) | Function |
|---|---|
| Tab | Moves the active cell one cell to the right. |

| Key(s) | Function |
| --- | --- |
| Shift+Tab | Moves the active cell one cell to the left. |
| Enter | Moves the active cell down one cell. |
| Shift+Enter | Moves the active cell up one cell. |
| Ctrl+. (period ) | Moves the active cell to the next corner of selection. |
| Ctrl+Tab | Moves the active cell to the next selected range. |
| Shift+Ctrl+Tab | Moves the active cell to the preceding selected range. |
| Shift+Backspace | Collapses the selection to the active cell. |

If you are using a mouse, hold down Ctrl and click the desired location.

# Using Editing Keys in the Formula Bar

At times, you may simply want to edit data or text in a cell rather than delete it or type over it.

The following keys move the cursor in Edit mode. Press F2 to enter Edit mode.

| Key(s) | Function |
| --- | --- |
| ←, →, ↑, or ↓ | Moves the cursor one character or one line in the direction of the arrow. |
| Home | Moves the cursor to the beginning of the line. |
| End | Moves the cursor to the end of the line. |
| Ctrl+← or Ctrl+→ | Moves the cursor one word at a time left or right. |

The following keys remove data in Edit mode:

| Key(s) | Function |
| --- | --- |
| Backspace | Deletes the character to the left of the cursor. |
| Del | Deletes the character to the right of the cursor. If characters are selected, Del deletes the selection. |
| Ctrl+Del | Deletes all characters from the cursor to the end of the line. |

## Using Formatting Keys

The formatting keys apply a specific format, such as bold, to the current cell or selection. You can use the following formatting keys:

| Key(s) | Function |
| --- | --- |
| Ctrl+1 | Applies normal format. |
| Ctrl+2 Ctrl+B | Applies or removes boldface. |
| Ctrl+3 Ctrl+I | Applies or removes italicizing. |
| Ctrl+4 Ctrl+U | Applies or removes underlining. |
| Ctrl+S | Selects the Style box. |
| Ctrl+Shift+~ | Specifies the general number format. |
| Ctrl+Shift+! | Specifies comma format with 2 decimal places [#,##0.00]. |
| Ctrl+Shift+# | Specifies date format [d-mmm-yy]. |

| Key(s) | Function |
|--------|----------|
| Ctrl+Shift+$ | Specifies currency format with 2 decimal places [$#,##0.00]. |
| Ctrl+Shift+% | Specifies percent format with 0 decimal places [0%]. |

# Using Function Keys

Function keys save you time when you edit cells, move between windows, save files, and get help. Your keyboard contains 10 or 12 function keys, labeled F1 through F10 or F1 through F12, respectively. Excel supports all 12 keys.

Following is a list of function keys and key combinations and the command equivalents:

| Key(s) | Command Equivalent |
|--------|--------------------|
| F1 | Help |
| Shift+F1 | Context-sensitive Help |
| Alt+F1 | File New (Chart) |
| Alt+Shift+F1 | File New (Worksheet) |
| Alt+Ctrl+F1 | File New (Macro sheet) |
| F2 | Edit formula in formula bar |
| Shift+F2 | Formula Note |
| Ctrl+F2 | Options Workspace; Info Window check box. |
| Alt+F2 | File Save As |
| Alt+Shift+F2 | File Save |
| Alt+Ctrl+F2 | File Open |

| Key(s) | Command Equivalent |
| --- | --- |
| Alt+Ctrl+ Shift+F2 | File Print |
| F3 | Formula Paste Name |
| Shift+F3 | Formula Paste Function |
| Ctrl+F3 | Formula Define Name |
| Ctrl+Shift+F3 | Formula Create Names |
| F4 | Formula Cell Reference (Absolute key) |
| Ctrl+F4 | Control Close (document window) |
| Alt+F4 | Control Close (application window) |
| F5 | Formula Goto |
| Shift+F5 | Formula Find (cell contents) |
| Ctrl+F5 | Control Restore (document window) |
| F6 | Next pane |
| Shift+F6 | Previous pane |
| Ctrl+F6 | Control Next Window |
| Ctrl+Shift+F6 | Previous document window |
| F7 | Formula Find (next occurrence) |
| Shift+F7 | Formula Find (previous occurrence) |
| Ctrl+F7 | Control Move (document window) |
| F8 | Extend mode (on/off) |
| Shift+F8 | Add mode (on/off) |
| Ctrl+F8 | Control Size (document window) |
| F9 | Options Calculation; Calc Now button |
| Shift+F9 | Options Calculation; Calc Document button |
| Ctrl+F9 | Control Minimize (document window) |

| Key(s) | Command Equivalent |
|---|---|
| F10 | Activate menu bar |
| Shift+F10 | Activate shortcut menu |
| Ctrl+F10 | Control Maximize (document window) |
| F11 | File New (chart) |
| Shift+F11 | File New (worksheet) |
| Ctrl+F11 | File New (macro sheet) |
| F12 | File Save As |
| Shift+F12 | File Save |
| Ctrl+F12 | File Open |
| Ctrl+Shift+F12 | File Print |

## Using Toolbars

The Standard Toolbar displays tools used for opening files, saving files, printing files, applying styles, changing font sizes, formatting and aligning cells, creating an outline, summing numbers in a range, and creating a chart on a worksheet. By default, only the Standard Toolbar appears on-screen when Excel starts. The Chart Toolbar displays by default when a chart is opened.

In addition to the Standard Toolbar, Excel 4.0 provides eight Toolbars that each contain a related group of tools. These Toolbars are Formatting, Utility, Chart, Drawing, Excel 3.0 Toolbar, Macro, Stop Recording, and Macro Paused. All , several, or just one Toolbar can be on-screen at any one time.

You can also create custom Toolbars that can include any tool; typically these Toolbars are more compatible with your work style and needs. You can create a whole new Toolbar or make changes to an existing Toolbar. In the Toolbars dialog box, after you type a name in the Toolbar Name box and choose Customize, a Categories list defines—by category—the available tools. The custom tools categories are File, Edit, Formula, Formatting, Text Formatting, Drawing, Macro, Charting, Utility, and Custom.

When you select a category, the tools available for that category appear under the Tools display area. To add a tool to a Toolbar, you simply drag the tool from the Tools display area and drop it on the on-screen Toolbar.

### To turn a Toolbar on or off

1. Press Alt, O, O or click the Options menu and select Toolbars.

2. Select the Toolbar from the Show Toolbars list, and click Show or Hide, depending on your task.

### The Standard Toolbar

Following is a list of each tool on the Standard Toolbar and a description of its purpose:

| Tool | Tool Name | Purpose |
|------|-----------|---------|
| | New Worksheet | Creates a new worksheet. |
| | Open File | Displays the File Open dialog box so that you can open an existing file. |
| | Save File | Saves the active file. |

| Tool | Tool Name | Purpose |
|------|-----------|---------|
| 🖨 | Print | Prints the active document. |
| ⬇ | Style Box | Applies a cell style to the selection or lets you define a style based on the current selection. |
| Σ | Auto Sum | Places a SUM formula in the active cell with a range based on the data above or to the left of the active cell. |
| **B** | Bold | Turns on or off bold formatting. |
| *I* | Italic | Turns on or off italic formatting. |
| A▲ | Increase Font Size | Increases the font size of the selection. |
| A▼ | Decrease Font Size | Decreases the font size of the selection. |
| ≡ | Left Align | Left-aligns the selection. |
| ≡ | Center | Centers the selection. |
| ≡ | Right Align | Right-aligns the selection. |
| ⊞ | Center Across Columns | Centers the text from one cell horizontally across selected columns. |

| Tool | Tool Name | Purpose |
|------|-----------|---------|
| | AutoFormat | Automatically formats a range of cells by recognizing header rows and columns, summary rows and columns, and other elements of a table. |
| | Outline Border | Adds a border around a cell or selection. |
| | Bottom Border | Adds a bottom border around a cell or selection. |
| | Copy | Copies a selection to the Clipboard. |
| | Paste | Pastes formats only from copied cells to selected cells. |
| | ChartWizard | Starts the ChartWizard so that you can edit an embedded chart or chart document or create a new chart as an embedded object on a worksheet. |
| | Help Tool | Adds a question mark to the mouse pointer. When you position the question mark over a command or cell and click, the Excel Help specific to that command or cell's contents appears. |

# COMMAND REFERENCE

The command reference is an alphabetical listing of all Microsoft Excel commands. The command name is followed by the purpose of the command and instructions for its use.

Throughout the command reference, keys that you type or letters that you press appear in **boldface blue** type. Any text, such as error messages, that appears on-screen is presented in a `special` typeface.

Remember that key combinations separated by a plus sign (+) indicate that you need to press down the first key, press the second key, and then release both keys. Key combinations separated by a comma (,) indicate that you must press and release the first key, and then press and release the second key.

# Chart Add (Delete) Arrow

### Purpose

Adds (or deletes) an arrow on a chart. Used to add (or delete) arrows of various sizes, colors, weights, and styles.

### To add an arrow

1. Press **Alt**, **C**, **R** or click the **C**hart menu and select Add A**r**row.

2. Use the Forma**t** Mo**v**e command or the mouse to move the arrow.

3. Use the Forma**t** Si**z**e command or the mouse to resize the arrow.

4. Use the Forma**t** **P**atterns command to format the arrow, or double-click the arrow to bring up the patterns dialog box.

### To delete an arrow

1. Select the arrow.

2. Press **Del**; press **Alt**, **C**, **R**; or click the **C**hart menu and select Delete A**r**row.

# Chart Add (Delete) Legend

### Purpose

Adds (or deletes) a legend on a chart. A legend identifies the different data series in the chart.

### To add a legend

1. Press **Alt**, **C**, **L** or click the **C**hart menu and select Add **L**egend. The legend appears on the right side of the chart.

2. Move the legend by using the Forma**t L**egend or Forma**t Mo**ve commands. You also can drag the legend with the mouse.

3. Format the legend using the Forma**t P**atterns command or double-click the legend to bring up the patterns dialog box.

### To delete a legend

Select the **C**hart Delete **L**egend command or select the legend and Press **Del**. Added legends assume the formatting of the deleted legend.

### Notes

The plot area of the chart resizes to make room for the legend.

The **P**atterns and **F**ont commands are available through the Forma**t L**egend dialog box, as well as through the Forma**t P**atterns command.

# Chart Add (Delete) Overlay

### Purpose

Overlays (or deletes) a second chart over the current (main) chart to create a combination chart. The data series are evenly divided between the main chart and overlay chart. If the number of data series is odd, the main chart includes the extra data series.

### To add an overlay

1. Press **Alt, C, O** or click the **C**hart menu and select Add **O**verlay.

2. Change the overlay's chart type and format by selecting the Forma**t O**verlay command.

### To delete the overlay

Select the **C**hart Delete **O**verlay command.

## Chart Attach Text

### Purpose

Inserts text near a chart object, such as the title, the axes, or a data series. If you move or resize a chart object, the text moves or resizes with it.

### To attach text

1. Press **Alt, C, T** or click the **C**hart menu and select Attach **T**ext. You also can click the right mouse button to bring up the shortcut menu and select Attach Text.

2. Select Chart **T**itle, **V**alue [Y] Axis, **C**ategory [X] Axis, Series and **D**ata Point, Overlay Value [**Y**] Axis, or Overlay Category [**X**] axis.

3. Press **Enter** or click **OK**.

4. In the formula bar, type the text you want to attach and press **Enter**.

5. Select Forma**t T**ext to format the text or double-click the text. You also can select Forma**t P**atterns to bring up the patterns dialog box.

### To add unattached text

1.  Make sure that no object is selected and that the formula bar is blank.

2.  In the formula bar, type the text you want to add and press Enter.

    The text appears in the center of the chart surrounded by black squares (called *handles*). To move the text with the mouse, click and drag the text; to use the keyboard, use the Format Move command.

### To edit text

1.  Select the text. The text appears in the formula bar.

2.  Press F2 or click the formula bar. Edit the text and press Enter.

    You can delete text by selecting it and pressing Del.

## Chart Axes

### Purpose

Hides or displays the category [X] axis, the value [Y] axis, or, if a 3-D graph, the value [Z] axis.

### To hide or display axes

1.  Press Alt, C, X or click the Chart menu and select Chart Axes. You also can click the right mouse button to bring up the shortcut menu, and then select Axes.

2. From the dialog box, select the axes you want to hide or display.

3. Press **Enter** or click **OK**.

### Note

When an axis is hidden, the plot area resizes to fill the extra space.

## Chart Calculate Now

### Purpose

When manual calculation is on, recalculates all open worksheets, and then redraws all open charts supported by those worksheets.

### To recalculate

Press **Alt**, **C**, **N**, press **F9**, or click the Chart menu and select Calculate Now.

## Chart Color Palette

### Purpose

Customizes colors in the color palette and copies color palettes between open documents.

### To change a color

1. Press **Alt**, **C**, **E** or click the Chart menu and select Color Palette.

2. Select a color in the palette and select the Edit command. Select another color to replace the color in the palette. Press Enter or click OK.

3. Press Enter or click OK.

### To copy a color palette

1. Press Alt, C, E or click the Chart menu and select the Color Palette command.

2. Press Alt+C or click the Copy Colors From drop-down list box to see all open documents.

3. To copy the color palette from an open document, select the document name. Press Enter or click OK.

### To reset the color palette

Select the Default button in the Color Palette dialog box. The color palette is reset to its original 16 colors.

## Chart Edit Series

### Purpose

Creates, edits or deletes a data series on an active chart.

### To create, edit, or delete data series

1. Press Alt, C, I or click the Chart menu and select Edit Series. You also can click the right mouse button to bring up the shortcut menu, and then select Edit Series.

2. Select the data series from the Series box. Select New Series to create a new data series.

3. Press Alt+E or click the Delete button to delete the selected data series.

4. Edit the formulas in the Name, X Labels, Y Values, or Z Values (3-D charts only) text boxes. Press Alt+D or click the Define button to plot the data series on the active chart.

5. Use Plot Order to define the order in which the selected data series is plotted on the chart. (You can plot up to 255 series).

6. Press Enter or click OK to accept the changes and close the dialog box.

# Chart Gridlines

### *Purpose*

Displays or hides major and minor gridlines attached to the category and value axes.

### *To display or hide gridlines*

1. Press Alt, C, G or click the Chart menu and select Gridlines. You also can click the right mouse button to bring up the shortcut menu, and then select Gridlines.

2. Set Category [X] Axis Major Gridlines, Category [X] Axis Minor Gridlines, Series [Y] Axis Major Gridlines, and/or Series [Y] Axis Minor Gridlines.

   If you have a 3-D graph, set Series [Z] Axis Major Gridlines and/or Series [Z] Axis Minor Gridlines, rather than setting Series [Y] Axis Gridlines.

3. Press Enter or click OK.

# Chart Protect Document

## *Purpose*

Protects (or unprotects) a chart's data series, formats, and window from change. Provides password protection.

## *To protect a chart*

1. Press Alt, C, P or click the Chart menu and select Protect Document.

2. Turn on Chart to protect the chart's data series and formats.

3. Turn on Windows to protect the chart's window screen position, size, and other characteristics.

4. Press Enter or click OK to turn on chart protection without a password.

5. Select Password and type a password of up to 16 characters.

6. Press Enter or click OK.

7. Verify the password, and then press Enter or click OK.

## *To unprotect a chart*

1. Press Alt, C, P or click the Chart menu and select the Unprotect Document command.

   If you did not password-protect the chart, you can alter the chart. If you did password-protect the chart, you must provide the password to alter the chart.

2. Type the password and press Enter or click OK.

If you do not enter the correct password, Excel beeps and displays an error message. Repeat steps 1 and 2.

## Chart Select Chart

### Purpose

Selects all elements of a chart, enabling the Format and Edit commands to affect all aspects of the chart.

### To select an entire chart

1. Press Alt, C, C or click the Chart menu and select Select Chart.

2. Use the Edit Clear command to delete the chart's data series or formats.

3. Use the Edit Copy command to copy the chart's data series or formats to the Clipboard.

4. Use the Format Font and Format Patterns commands to change the appearance of the chart.

5. To unselect the chart, press Esc.

## Chart Select Plot Area

### Purpose

Selects a chart's plot area so that any changes made using Format Patterns will affect all elements in the area bounded by the axes.

### To select the plot area

1. Press **Alt**, **C**, **A** or click the Chart menu and select Select Plot Area.

2. Use the Format Patterns command to change the border style, border color, border weight, background pattern, background color, or foreground color of the plot area.

3. To unselect the chart, press **Esc**. Press an arrow key or click the mouse to select an object in the chart rather than the entire chart.

# Chart Spelling

### Purpose

Checks the spelling of all chart text that is not linked to a worksheet cell.

### To check spelling

1. Press **Alt**, **C**, **S** or click the Chart menu and select Spelling.

   Excel begins checking the spelling of the text in the chart.

2. Choose the appropriate options for the misspelled word:

   Change To/Suggestions lists the word Excel believes you are trying to use. You can leave the default suggestion, select another word in the suggestion list, or type a word into the box.

   Add Words To adds the identified word to the dictionary shown in the Add Words To box. By default, CUSTOM.DIC is the dictionary in the Add Words To box.

Ignore leaves the selected word unchanged.

Ignore All leaves the selected word unchanged throughout the selection, worksheet, or macro sheet.

Change changes the selected word to the word in the Change To box.

Change All changes the selected word to the word in the Change To box throughout the selection, worksheet, or macro sheet.

Add adds the selected word to the dictionary in the Add Words To box.

Suggestions displays a list of proposed suggestions in the Suggestions list box for a word typed into the Change To box.

Ignore Words in UPPERCASE tells the spelling checker to ignore words that contain only capital letters.

Always Suggest causes a list of suggested words to display in the Suggestions box every time Excel finds a misspelled word.

Cancel/Close closes the dialog box. Cancel changes to Close if you add a word to a dictionary or change a misspelled word.

3. Press **Enter** or click **OK**.

# Control Close

### *Purpose*

Closes the active application or document window.

### *To close an application window*

Press **Alt**, **space bar**, **C** or **Alt+F4**. You also can click the Application Control menu box and select **C**lose.

### *To close a document window*

Press Alt, -, C or Ctrl+F4. You also can click the
Document Control menu and select Close.

## Control Maximize

### *Purpose*

Expands the active application or document window
to fill the screen space.

### *To expand an application window*

Press Alt, space bar, X; click the Application Control
menu and select Maximize; or click the Maximize
icon in the upper right corner of the application
window.

### *To expand a document window*

Press Alt, -, X; press Ctrl+F10; click the Document
Control menu and select Maximize; or click the
Maximize icon in the upper right corner of the
document window. In document windows you
maximize, the Control menu dash that normally
appears at the document's top left corner changes
to a slightly smaller dash to the left of the menu.

### *To restore a window*

Select Control Restore. The window returns to its
preceding size and location.

# Control Minimize

### Purpose

Collapses the active application or document window to an icon at the bottom of the screen so that you have more room on-screen.

### To collapse an application window

Press Alt, space bar, N; click the Application Control menu and select Minimize; or click the Minimize icon in the upper right corner of the application window.

To collapse a document window, press Alt, -, N; press Ctrl+F9; click the Document Control menu and select Minimize; or click the minimize icon in the upper right corner of the document window.

### To restore a window

Select Control Restore. The window returns to its previous size and location.

# Control Move

### Purpose

Moves the active application or document window. The Control Move command is available only when the window is in the restored position.

### *To move an application window*

1. Press **Alt**, **space bar**, **M** or click the Application Control menu and select **Move**.

2. Use the arrow keys to move the window. To move the window in smaller increments, press **Ctrl** and an arrow key.

3. After you position the window, press **Enter**.

### *To move a document window*

1. Press **Alt**, **-**, **M**; press **Ctrl+F7**; or click the Document Control menu and select **Move**.

2. Press the arrow keys to move the window. To move the window in smaller increments, press **Ctrl** and the appropriate arrow key.

3. After you position the window, press **Enter**.

### *To use the mouse to move a window*

Drag the title bar of the window to move the window.

## Control Next Window

### *Purpose*

Switches to the next open document window.

### *To switch to the next window*

Press **Alt**, **–**, **T**; press **Ctrl+F6**; or click the Document Control menu and select Next Window.

# Control Restore

### Purpose

Restores an application or document window to its preceding size and location, but does not affect changes made by the Control Size and Control Move commands.

### To restore an application window

Press **Alt**, **space bar**, **R**; click the Application Control menu and select **Restore**; or click the Restore icon in the upper right corner of the application window.

### To restore a document window

Press **Alt**, **-**, **R**; press **Ctrl+F5**; click the Document Control menu and select **Restore**; or click the Restore icon in the upper right corner of the document window.

# Control Run

### Purpose

Runs the Clipboard, the Control Panel, the Macro Translator, or the Dialog Editor.

### To operate these features

1. Press **Alt**, **space bar**, **U** or click the Application Control menu and select **Run**.

2. Select the Clipboard to see its contents, the Control Panel to adjust system settings, the Macro Translator to convert Lotus 1-2-3 macros to Excel macros, or the Dialog Editor to create custom dialog boxes.

3. Press Enter or click OK.

## Control Size

### *Purpose*

Changes the size of the active application or document window. This command is available only when the window is in the restored position.

### *To change the size of an application window*

1. Press Alt, space bar, S or click the Application Control menu and select Size.

2. Use the arrow keys to resize the window. To resize the window in smaller increments, press Ctrl and the appropriate arrow key.

3. When the window is the desired size, press Enter.

### *To change the size of a document window*

1. Press Alt, –, S; press Ctrl+F8; or click the Document Control menu and select Size.

2. Use the arrow keys to resize the window. To resize the window in smaller increments, press Ctrl and the appropriate arrow key.

3. When the window is the size you want, press Enter.

### To use the mouse to change the size of a window

Drag the window border. The mouse pointer changes to a two-headed arrow when positioned on the window border, and the window is resized.

## Control Split

### Purpose

Divides the active document window into panes and creates separate scrolls for each pane. This command is available only for worksheets and macro sheets.

### To use the keyboard to divide the document window

1. Press Alt, -, P or click the Document Control menu and select Split.

2. Press the arrow keys to move the split panes pointer until the division is where you want it.

3. Press Enter.

### To use the mouse to divide the document window

Drag the split bars from the solid black rectangles that appear next to the scroll arrows (at the window's bottom left and top right corners). The mouse pointer changes shape when positioned on the split bars.

# Control Switch To

### Purpose

Displays the Task List and all open applications. Enables you to switch to another open application.

### To switch to another application

1. Press **Alt**, **space bar**, **W**; click the Application Control menu and select Switch To; or press **Ctrl+Esc**.

   The Task List dialog box appears.

2. From the list, select the application to switch to.

3. Press **Alt+S**, click the Switch To button, or double-click the application name.

# Data Consolidate

### Purpose

Consolidates data from multiple ranges or multiple sheets into a single range.

### To consolidate data

1. Select the destination area for the consolidated data. The destination area can be a single cell, a range of cells, a single column, or a single row.

2. Press **Alt**, **D**, **N** or click the Data menu and select Consolidate.

3. Select the function you want to use to consolidate data. The default function is SUM.

4. Select the Top Row check box or the Left Column check box if you want to consolidate data by category labels. (If a category check box is turned off, that data is consolidated by position.)

5. Press Alt+R or click the Reference text box.

6. Select the data you want to consolidate.

7. Press Alt+A or click the Add button to add a range to the All References list. You can specify up to 255 ranges to consolidate. If you want to delete a reference, select the reference from the All References list and press Alt+D or click the Delete button.

8. Press Alt+S or click the Create Links to Source Data check box if you want Excel to update the data in the destination area when the source data changes.

9. Press Enter or click OK to consolidate data. Press Alt+F4, click the Close button, or press Esc to close the Consolidate dialog box without consolidating data.

## Data Delete

### *Purpose*

Erases database records that match the criteria in the criteria range and moves subsequent records to fill the empty space. This command has no effect on worksheet data outside the database.

**CAUTION:** Because you cannot undo the effects of the Data Delete command, be careful of what you specify for elimination. Do not include blank rows in the criteria range because the command then matches and deletes all records in the database.

### To delete specified data

1. Use the Data Set Database and Data Set Criteria commands to define your database range and criteria range.

2. Enter your criteria.

3. Use the Data Find command to preview the data you want to delete.

4. Press Alt, D, D or click the Data menu and select Delete. Press Enter or click OK to delete the records permanently.

## Data Extract

### Purpose

Copies into the extract range database records that match specified criteria.

**CAUTION:** Because you cannot reverse the clearing of cell contents with Edit Undo, use the Extract command with caution.

## To extract data

1. Use the Data Set Database, and Data Set Criteria commands to define your database range and criteria range.

2. Enter your criteria.

3. Use the Data Set Extract command to define your extract range. The first row of the range should contain the names of the database fields you want to work with.

   If you select the first row and the rows below it, the extracted data is limited to only those rows, erasing any existing data. Excel copies as much data as it can and then displays a message warning that the extract range is full.

   If you select only the first row, the extract range is unlimited and all cells below it are defined as part of the extract range. All the cells are cleared of data, whether or not data copies to them.

4. Press Alt, D, E or click the Data menu and select the Extract command.

   You do not have to define an extract range with Data Set Extract to extract database records. You can select an extract range before choosing the Data Extract command.

5. Select whether to extract Unique Records Only. This setting filters out duplicate database records.

6. Press Enter or click OK.

   The records matching your criteria copy to the extract range. Excel extracts only the value of the formula from records containing formulas.

# Data Find (Exit Find)

## *Purpose*

Selects records in the database that match the criteria in the criteria range.

## *To find data*

1. Use the Data Set Database and Data Set Criteria commands to define your database range and criteria range.

2. Enter your criteria. One of the following operators must precede the criteria: =, >, <, >=, <=, or <>. If you omit the operator, Excel uses =.

3. Press Alt, D, F, or click the Data menu and select Find. For a backward search, press Shift as you select Find.

   If the active cell is outside the database when you execute the command, Excel selects the first record that matches the criteria. If the active cell is in the database, Excel selects the first record following the active cell that matches the criteria. Also, the scroll bars become striped to show that you are in Find mode.

4. Move across fields in the selected record by pressing Tab or Enter to go right and Shift+Tab or Shift+Enter to go left.

5. Move to the next or preceding matching record by pressing ↓ or ↑ or clicking the down or up scroll arrows. Excel beeps when it finds no more matches.

6. Move to the next or preceding matching record at least a page away by pressing PgDn or PgUp or by clicking below or above the scroll box. Excel beeps when it finds no more matches.

7. Scroll the screen up to the width of the database by pressing ← or → or by dragging the
scroll box.

8. When you finish examining the matched
records, press Esc, select the Data Exit Find
command, or click a cell outside the database.
The scroll bars return to normal.

## Data Form

### Purpose

Enables you to view, find, edit, add, and delete
database records, thus offering an alternative to
many of the Data menu commands.

### To access the database form

1. Define your database range using the Data Set
Database command.

2. Press Alt, D, O, or click the Data menu and
select the Form command.

The left side of the dialog box contains a list of
all database field names. To the right of each
field name is its entry for the first record. To
the right of the record entries are the command buttons.

3. To move among entries, use the following
keys:

| | |
|---|---|
| Tab | Moves forward among record entries and command buttons. |
| Shift+Tab | Moves backward among record entries and command buttons. |
| Enter | Moves to the top of the next record. |

| Shift+Enter | Moves to the top of the preced- ing record. |
| Ctrl+PgUp | Moves to the first record in the database. |
| Ctrl+PgDn | Moves to the end of the database and creates a new record. |
| ↓ | Moves to the same field in the next record. |
| ↑ | Moves to the same field in the preceding record. |

## To add new records

1. Press Alt, D, O or click the Data menu and select Form.

2. Select New, press Ctrl+PgDn, or click and drag the center scroll box to the bottom of the scroll bar.

3. Enter new data into the appropriate fields.

4. Press Enter to move to the next empty record.

5. Press Alt+F4 or click Close to close.

## To remove a record

1. Press Alt, D, O or click the Data menu and select Form.

2. Move to the record.

3. Select Delete, and then press Enter or click OK. The record is permanently deleted, and Excel renumbers all subsequent records.

4. Press Alt+F4 or click Close.

### To change a field entry

1. Press **Alt**, **D**, **O** or click the **D**ata menu and select **F**orm.

2. Select and edit the database field.

3. If you edit the database, you can select **Re**store to remove changes and restore the edited field to its original state.

4. Press Alt+F4 or click **C**lose.

### To find specific records

1. Press **Alt**, **D**, **O** or click the **D**ata menu and select **F**orm.

2. Select **C**riteria to display criteria options.

3. Select **C**lear to remove the current criteria.

4. Enter criteria for the appropriate field(s). (This criteria is separate from the criteria range, which Data Form ignores.) Precede the criteria with one of the following operators: =, >, <, >=, <=, or <>. If you omit the operator, Excel uses =. Press **Enter** to find the first record that matches the criteria.

5. Select Find Next to display the next matching record or Find Prev to find the preceding matching record.

6. Press **Alt**+F4 or click **C**lose.

## Data Parse

### Purpose

Distributes imported cell contents across multiple columns (typically needed to correct the results of importing ASCII data).

### *To distribute data across columns*

1. Select the cells that contain multiple data.

2. Press **Alt**, **D**, **P**, or click the Data menu and select the **P**arse command.

   The data in the first cell of your range appears on the **P**arse Line. The cell address of the first cell of your range appears in the **D**estination box.

3. If you want the data to begin separating into cells beginning at a different location, enter a new location.

4. Select **C**lear to clear the brackets indicating where the data should be split up into separate columns.

5. Select **G**uess to have Excel insert brackets in the places it guesses for splitting the data.

6. Edit the **P**arse Line by inserting and deleting brackets.

7. Press **Enter** or click **OK**.

   Selected cells are parsed based on the bracket placements in the first cell.

## Data Series

### *Purpose*

Fills the selected range with a series of numbers or dates based on the value in the first cell and your command settings.

### To fill a range with a series of numbers or dates

1. Enter starting values in the first row or first column of the range.

2. Select the range.

3. Press **Alt**, **D**, **R**, or click the **D**ata menu and select Series.

4. Select whether to fill the range based on the starting values in its **R**ows or in its **C**olumns.

5. Enter the **S**tep Value, which is the amount by which each successive cell in the range increases.

6. Select **L**inear to add the **S**tep Value to each successive cell, **G**rowth to multiply the **S**tep Value by each successive cell, **D**ate to generate a series of numeric dates, or Auto**F**ill to fill blank cells in a selection with a series based on data included in the selection.

7. If you select **D**ate, also select whether you want to progress the dates by D**a**y, **W**eekday, **M**onth, or **Y**ear.

8. Optionally, enter a St**o**p Value to set a number-generation ceiling, unless you want numbers generated to the end of the range.

9. Press **Enter** or click **OK**.

## Data Set Criteria

### Purpose

Defines the range of cells containing the database criteria.

### To define criteria

1.  Select a range of cells to hold the database criteria. Place the criteria range directly above the database to keep the criteria in view.

    The range must be at least two rows. The first row contains the names of the database fields and the following row(s) contain the criteria.

    Precede the criteria with one of the following operators: =, >, <, >=, <=, or <>. If you omit the operator, Excel uses =.

2.  Press **Alt**, **D**, **C**, or click the **D**ata menu and select Set **C**riteria.

    Excel assigns the name *Criteria* to the range and establishes the range as the criteria range for data operations.

    You can define only one criteria range at a time in a worksheet; however, you can set up multiple ranges in the criteria format, and then use this command to reassign the criteria definition quickly to any of the ranges.

    Refer to criteria in other worksheets by using the Formula Define Name command to insert the name of the other worksheet and an exclamation point in front of the criteria name.

## Data Set Database

### Purpose

Defines the range of cells comprising the database.

### To define a database

1.  Select a range of cells to hold the database. Place the database just below the criteria range to keep the criteria in view.

The cells can be blank or nonblank. The range should include three rows (but must at least include the field name row and one data or blank row). The first row must contain the field names. The following row(s) contain database records and/or a blank row. You include a blank row so that the database range will redefine automatically as it grows.

2. Press **Alt**, **D**, **B**, or click the **D**ata menu and select Set Database.

Excel assigns the name *Database* to the range and establishes the range as the database range for data operations.

You can define only one database range at a time in a worksheet; however, you can set up multiple database ranges, and then use this command to reassign the database definition quickly to any of the named ranges.

Refer to databases in other worksheets by using the Formula Define Name command to insert the name of the other worksheet and an exclamation point in front of the database name.

## Data Set Extract

### *Purpose*

Defines the selected cells as the extract range for copying records that match the criteria.

### *To define an extract range*

1. Select a range of cells to hold the copied records that match the criteria defined in the criteria range.

The extract range must be outside your database and can contain only field names, or field names and selected cells below the field names that will contain the copied data.

If you select the first row and any rows below the first row, the extracted data is limited to those rows only and clears those rows of data. Excel copies as much data as space permits and then displays a message warning that the extract range is full.

> **CAUTION:** If you select only the first row of field names, the extract range is unlimited and all cells below are defined as part of the extract range.The cells are cleared of data, whether or not data copies to them. You cannot reverse this clearing with Edit Undo, so use this command with caution.

2.  Press **Alt**, **D**, **X** or click the **Data** menu and select Set Extract.

    Excel defines the extract range and names the range *Extract*.

# Data Sort

## *Purpose*

Organizes selected records based on a sort key row or column.

## *To sort data*

1.  After defining the database range using the Data Set Database command, select either all the database records or only the records you want to sort. Do not include the field names.

2. Press **Alt**, **D**, **S**, or click the **D**ata menu and select the **S**ort command.

3. Choose to sort by **R**ows or **C**olumns.

4. Enter the **1**st Key sort. If you select **R**ows in step 3, specify a column you want to sort by. If you select **C**olumns in step 3, specify a row you want to sort by.

5. Choose whether to sort by **A**scending or **De**scending order.

6. If necessary, enter a **2**nd or **3**rd sort key.

7. Press **Enter** or click **OK**.

## Data Table

### Purpose

Substitutes values from a selected range for the value in a specified cell, and then generates a "what if" table of the results from a specified formula or formulas.

### To create a single-input table

1. In a single row or single column, create a list of values to be substituted for the value in the input cell.

2. The values may be in a column. If so, in the row above the first value and one cell to the right of the column of values, enter the formula that refers to the input cell. If the values are in a row, enter the formula in the column to the left of the first value and one cell below the row of values.

3. Select the rectangular range that contains the formula and the list of values.

4. Press **Alt**, **D**, **T**, or click the **D**ata menu and select **T**able.

5. Enter the cell reference in which you want to substitute the list of values. If the values are in a row, enter the reference in the **R**ow Input Cell box. If the values are in a column, enter the reference in the **C**olumn Input Cell box.

6. Press **Enter** or click **OK**.

### *To create a two-input table*

1. In a cell directly above a column of values and to the left of a row of values, enter the formula that refers to the two input cells.

2. Select the range that includes the formula (in the upper left corner) and the two lists of values.

3. Press **Alt**, **D**, **T**, or click the **D**ata menu and select **T**able.

4. Enter the cell references in which you want to substitute the list of values. For values in the row, enter the cell reference in the **R**ow Input Cell box. For values in the column, enter the cell reference in the **C**olumn Input Cell box.

5. Press **Enter** or click **OK**.

## Edit Clear

### *Purpose*

Removes cell data, formulas, formats, or notes from the selected cells.

**CAUTION:** Do not confuse Edit Clear with Edit Delete. Edit Clear clears the cells contents and formatting; Edit Delete shifts cells to eliminate the deleted cell.

## To clear a cell or range

1. Select the cell or range you want to clear.

2. Press Alt, E, E; press Del; or click the Edit menu and select Clear. You also can click the right mouse button to bring up the shortcut menu and then select Clear.

3. If a dialog box appears, select to clear All, Formats, Formulas, or Notes. Then press Enter or click OK.

   For charts, select Series or Formats, and then press Enter or click OK.

## Note

In formulas, a cleared cell has a value of zero.

# Edit Copy

## Purpose

Copies a selection to the Clipboard. You can copy a range of cells, characters from the formula bar, or an entire chart.

## *To copy a selection to the Clipboard*

1. Select a cell, a range of cells, characters from the formula bar, or an entire chart.

2. Press **Alt, E, C**; press **Ctrl+C**, press **Ctrl+Ins**; or click the **Edit** menu and select **Copy**. You can also click the right mouse button to bring up the shortcut menu and select Copy.

   A marquee appears around your selection, and the data and formatting of your selection copies to the Clipboard.

3. Select a single destination cell.

4. To make only one copy, press **Enter**.

   To make multiple copies, use the **Edit Paste** or **Edit Paste Special** command. Then press **Esc** to clear the marquee.

## *Notes*

Excel also provides the following quick copy alternatives:

| Key(s) | Function |
|--------|----------|
| **Ctrl+'** | Copies the formula from the cell above. |
| **Ctrl+"** | Copies the value from the cell above. |
| **Ctrl+Enter** | Copies data entered in the formula bar to a range of selected cells, filling the range. |

See also *Edit Fill Down (Up)* and *Edit Fill Right (Left)*.

## Edit Copy Picture

### Purpose

Copies a pictorial representation of a selection to the Clipboard for use in Excel or another application.

### To copy a selection to the Clipboard

1. Select the range or chart you want to copy. (The selection restrictions on Edit Copy do not apply here.)

2. Press Alt, Shift+E, C. You also can press Shift, click the Edit menu, and select Copy Picture.

3. Select whether you want the picture's appearance As Shown on Screen or As Shown when Printed. In a chart, you also need to select the same options for the picture's size.

4. If applicable, select the picture format. (The picture formats vary according to the type of graphic you are copying.)

5. Press Enter or click OK.

6. Select the destination and use the Edit Paste command to insert the picture.

## Edit Cut

### Purpose

Moves the selected data and formatting to the Clipboard for use in another destination. In a chart, the Edit Cut command is available only when characters are selected in the formula bar.

### *To move a selection to the Clipboard*

1. In a worksheet or macro sheet, select a cell, range of cells, or characters from the formula bar. In a chart, select characters from the formula bar.

2. Press Alt, E, T; press Shift+Del; press Ctrl+X; or click the Edit menu and select Cut. You also can click the right mouse button to bring up the shortcut menu and select Cut.

   A marquee appears around the selection, and the data and formatting of your selection are copied to the Clipboard.

3. Select a single destination cell and press Enter to move the selected data and formatting to the new destination. (Select a single destination cell rather than a range to avoid problems with ranges that are not the same size.)

   If you select characters from the formula bar and select the Edit Cut command, the characters are moved to the Clipboard. Select a single destination cell and select the Edit Paste command. The characters appear in the selected cell. A copy of the characters remains on the Clipboard, enabling you to make multiple copies.

### *Note*

Do not confuse this command with Edit Delete or Edit Clear, which remove—rather than move—data.

# Edit Delete

### *Purpose*

Removes specified cells, rows, or columns (and all
associated data and formatting) from the worksheet,
shifting surrounding cells to fill the space.

### *To delete cells, rows, or columns*

1. Select the cells, rows, or columns you want to
   delete.

2. Press **Alt, E, D**; press **Ctrl+-** (hyphen); or click
   the Edit menu and select Delete. You also can
   click the right mouse button to bring up the
   shortcut menu and select Delete.

3. Select the Shift Cells Left, Shift Cells Up, Entire
   Row, or Entire Column button, and then press
   **Enter** or click **OK**.

   In step 1, if you select an entire column or row
   rather than a cell or range, Excel automatically
   shifts surrounding columns or rows to fill the
   deleted column or row when you select the
   Edit Delete command.

   Formulas that refer to the deleted cells cannot
   locate the cells and display the error value
   #REF!.

### *Note*

See also *Edit Clear*, which removes a cell's data,
formatting, and notes, but leaves the cell in place.

# Edit Fill Down (Up)

## *Purpose*

Copies the data and the formats of the top (or bottom) of a range into the rest of the range.

## *To fill a range*

1. Select one or more ranges.
2. To fill down, press **Alt, E, W**; **Ctrl+D**; or **Ctrl+<**. You also can click the Edit menu and select Fill Down.

   To fill up, press **Alt, Shift+E, W**; or press down **Shift**, click the Edit menu, and select Fill Up(**w**).

The data and formats of the top (or bottom) of your range(s) copy into the selected cells below (or above) them. The ranges remain selected for further commands.

## *Notes*

Copied data replaces existing cell contents.

See also *Edit Copy*.

# Edit Fill Group

## *Purpose*

Copies the contents of the range of cells selected on an active worksheet to the same range of cells in all other sheets in the workgroup.

### *To fill a workgroup*

1. Press **Alt**, **O**, **G** or click the **O**ptions menu and select **G**roup Edit.

   Define a workgroup by selecting the open worksheets or macro sheets that you want to include in your workgroup.

2. Select a range in the active worksheet that you want to copy to the same range in all the sheets in the workgroup.

3. Press **Alt**, **E**, **G**, or click the **E**dit menu and select Fill **G**roup.

4. Select the **A**ll, For**m**ulas, or Forma**t**s button to copy all data and formats, only data, or only formats, respectively.

5. Press **Enter** or click **OK**.

### *Note*

This command has no effect on the range you are copying, but it does erase the destination cells.

## Edit Fill Right (Left)

### *Purpose*

Copies the data and the formats of the right (or left) column of a range into the rest of the range.

### *To fill a range*

1. Select one or more ranges.

2. To fill right, press **Alt**, **E**, **H**; press **Ctrl+R** or **Ctrl+>**; or click the **E**dit menu and select Fill **R**ight.

To fill left, press Alt, Shift+E, H; or press down Shift, click the Edit menu, and select Fill Left(h).

The data and formats of the right (or left) column of your range(s) copy into the selected cells to the left (or right). The ranges remain selected for further commands.

### Notes

Copied data replaces existing cell contents.

See also *Edit Copy*.

## Edit Insert

### Purpose

Inserts a blank cell or range, pushing existing cells to the right or down. Formulas that refer to the moved cells are revised to correspond to the new location.

### To insert a blank cell or range

1. Select a range the size of the cells you want to insert.

2. Press Alt, E, I; press Ctrl++; or click the Edit menu and select Insert. You also can click the right mouse button to bring up the shortcut menu and select Insert.

3. Select the Shift Cells Right, Shift Cells Down, Entire Row, or Entire Column button, and then press Enter or click OK.

*Note*

If you select an entire column or row rather than a cell or range, Excel automatically shifts surrounding columns or rows to insert the new column or row.

## Edit Insert Object

*Purpose*

Inserts an embedded object into a worksheet.

*To insert an object*

1. Select a cell in the area you want to insert the object. Objects insert into the worksheet at various sizes, depending on the application and the object you insert.

2. Press **Alt**, **E**, **O**, or click the **E**dit menu and select Insert **O**bject.

3. Select an object from the **O**bject Type list. The objects you see in the list depend on the applications you have installed. For instance, if you installed the Paintbrush program when you installed Windows, one of the objects will be Paintbrush Picture.

4. Press **Enter** or click **OK** to open the application you selected. If you selected Paintbrush Picture, for example, the Windows Paintbrush program opens.

   Create your object, and then choose File **U**pdate. File **U**pdate inserts the object into Excel.

   Switch back to Excel. The object you inserted appears embedded in the worksheet. The function =EMBED (*"objectname"*) appears in the formula bar when you activate the cell into which you inserted the object. (*Objectname* is the name of the inserted object.)

*Note*

You can edit the object by double-clicking it, which opens the application from which you created it.

# Edit Insert Paste

*Purpose*

Inserts the contents of the Clipboard between existing cells. The existing cells shift to accommodate the inserted cells.

*To paste a selection between cells*

1. Use **Edit Copy** or **Edit Cut** from within Excel or a comparable command from another application to insert information on the Clipboard. Examine the Clipboard with the Control Run command to make sure that the Clipboard contains the information you want.

2. Select a single cell and either press **Alt**, **E**, **I** or click the **Edit** menu and select **Insert Paste**. (When you copy or cut a selection using the Copy or Cut command, the Insert command changes to Insert Paste.)

3. Select Shift Cells **Right** to shift the existing cells to the right when inserting. Select Shift Cells **Down** to shift the existing cells down when inserting.

*Note*

If you cut or copy an entire row and then choose Insert Paste, the new row is inserted above the selected row. If you cut or copy an entire column and then choose Insert Paste, the new column is inserted to the left of the selected column.

## Edit Paste

### Purpose

Pastes a copy of the Clipboard's contents in a specific location. Precede this command with one of Excel's Edit commands or a comparable command from another application.

### To paste a selection

1. Use Edit Copy or Edit Cut from within Excel or a comparable command from another application to insert information on the Clipboard.

2. Select a single cell. Then press Alt, E, P; press Shift+Ins; press Ctrl+V; or click the Edit menu and select Paste. You also can click the right mouse button to bring up the shortcut menu and select Paste. The copy appears in the new location.

## Edit Paste Link

### Purpose

Pastes data with absolute references that refer to a cell or range copied to the Clipboard. A change in the original mirrors in its copies. Generally, you precede this command with the Edit Copy or Edit Cut command or a comparable command from another application.

### To paste and link a selection

1. Use **E**dit **C**opy or **E**dit **C**ut from within Excel or a comparable command from another application to insert information on the Clipboard.

2. Select the location in which you want to link the copied data or chart. If the selected range is not as large as the copied range, only the selected cells are filled.

3. Press **Alt**, **E**, **L**, or click the **E**dit menu and select Paste **L**ink. Excel inserts the absolute reference formula(s).

### Note

In most cases (except **E**dit **C**ut) you can make multiple copies. If you copy more than one cell, the command pastes an array.

## Edit Paste Picture

### Purpose

Pastes the contents of the Clipboard as a picture into a Microsoft Excel worksheet or macro sheet.

### To paste a picture into a worksheet

1. Use the **E**dit **C**opy command to copy a selection to the Clipboard.

2. Select the location in which you want to paste the copied data as a picture.

3. Press **Alt**, **Shift**+**E**, **P**; or press down **Shift**, click the **E**dit menu, and select **P**aste Picture.

# Edit Paste Picture Link

### Purpose

Pastes the contents of the Clipboard as a picture into a Microsoft Excel document and creates a link between the picture and the source data.

### To paste a picture into a worksheet

1. Select the location in which you want to paste the picture.

2. Press Alt, Shift+E, L; or press Shift, click the Edit menu, and select Paste Picture Link.

### Notes

When the source document changes, the pasted picture reflects those changes.

You can move and size a linked picture as you would any other graphic object.

# Edit Paste Special

### Purpose

Pastes data on the Clipboard and offers various pasting options for combining copied data with data in the destination cells. Precede this command with the Edit Copy command or a comparable command from another application.

## *To paste and combine a selection*

1. Use Edit Copy from within Excel or a comparable command from another application to insert information on the Clipboard.

2. Select the location where you want to paste the copied data.

3. Press Alt, E, S, or click the Edit menu and select Paste Special.

4. A dialog box appears, offering the following pasting options: All, Formulas, Values, Formats, and Notes.

   If you choose All, Formulas, or Values, specify how you want to combine the copied data with the destination cells. The options are: None, which replaces the paste area data with the copied data; Add, which adds the copied data to the paste area data; Subtract, which subtracts the copied data from the paste area data; Multiply, which multiplies the copied data and the paste area data; and Divide, which divides the paste area data by the copied data.

5. Turn on Skip Blanks if you don't want to copy blank cells from the Clipboard.

6. Turn on Transpose to switch the orientation of the copied data.

7. Press Enter or click OK.

## *Notes*

Use this command to format new worksheets with a variety of cell properties you created for an existing worksheet.

Use this command to convert formulas to values by copying, selecting the Values option, and then pasting the copies over the formulas.

## Edit Repeat

### *Purpose*

Repeats certain Excel operations.

### *To repeat an operation*

1. Perform an Excel operation that **R**epeat can perform. (For example, apply a format to a cell and then move to another cell to repeat applying the format.)

   The message Can't Repeat (dimmed) appears on the **E**dit menu if the operation cannot be performed by **R**epeat.

2. Press **Alt**, **E**, **R**; press **Alt+Enter**; or click the **E**dit menu and select **R**epeat.

   The operation can repeat until you do another operation.

## Edit Undo

### *Purpose*

Reverses many Excel operations, including entering or editing worksheet data, all **E**dit commands, and the Fo**r**mula **R**eplace, Format **J**ustify, **D**ata **P**arse, and **D**ata **S**ort commands. You can undo only the most recent operation.

### *To reverse an operation*

1. Perform an Excel operation that **U**ndo can reverse.

2. Press **Alt**, **E**, **U**; **Alt+Backspace**; or **Ctrl+Z**. You also can click the **E**dit menu and select **U**ndo. The document appears the way it was before the operation.

### Notes

The **U**ndo command actually appears as **U**ndo Paste, **U**ndo Copy, or **U**ndo Sort, depending on what you are undoing.

If you want the document as it was after the operation, immediately select Redo (**U**), which replaces **U**ndo on the **E**dit menu.

## File Activate File

### Purpose

Lists the last four active Excel files and enables you to open the file.

### To activate a file

1. Press **Alt**, **F** or click the **F**ile menu to display the last four opened Excel files.

2. Open a file by typing the number to the left of the file name or by clicking the file name.

## File Close

### Purpose

Closes the active document and its window(s).

> **CAUTION:** Be sure to save your documents before closing to avoid losing changes.

### To close a file

1. Press **Alt, F, C**, or click the **F**ile menu and select **C**lose.

2. If the document has unsaved changes, Excel asks whether you want to save the file with the changes you made since you opened it. Select **Y**es to save the document and close the window(s), **N**o to abandon your changes and close the window(s), or Cancel (by pressing **Esc** or clicking the Cancel button) to return to the document as if you had not selected **F**ile **C**lose.

# File Close All

### Purpose

Closes all open documents and their windows.

### To close all files

1. Press **Alt, Shift+F, C**; or press down **Shift**, click the **F**ile menu, and select **C**lose All.

2. If a document has unsaved changes, Excel asks whether you want to save the file with the changes you made since you opened it. Select **Y**es to save the document or select **N**o to abandon your changes. Excel prompts you to save every open document with unsaved changes.

If you select Cancel (by pressing **Esc** or
clicking the Cancel button) at any point, the
entire operation is canceled. You remain in
Excel, no files close, and you return to the
active document. The files you save before
you select Cancel remain saved.

## File Delete

### *Purpose*

Permanently deletes a file from disk.

### *To delete a file*

1. Press **Alt**, **F**, **D**, or click the **F**ile menu and
   select the **D**elete command.

   Files in the current directory appear in the
   **F**iles list box. Available directories appear in
   the **D**irectories list box. Available drives appear in the Dri**v**es list box.

2. Scroll through the **F**iles list with the scroll bar
   to select a file name, or type the name in the
   File **N**ame text box.

3. Press **Enter** or click **OK**. Press **Enter** or click
   Yes to confirm your choice.

4. After deleting files, press **Esc** or click Close to
   close the **D**elete dialog box.

## File Exit

### Purpose

Closes open documents and exits Excel.

### To close all files and exit Excel

1. Press Alt, F, X; press Alt+F4; or click the File menu and select Exit.

   To close all documents but remain in Excel, press down Shift, and select Close All from the File menu.

2. If a document has unsaved changes, Excel asks whether you want to save the file with your changes. Select Yes to save the document or select No to abandon your changes. Excel prompts you to save every open document with unsaved changes.

   If you select Cancel (by pressing Esc or clicking the Cancel button) at any point, the entire operation is canceled. You remain in Excel, no files close, and you return to the active document. The files you save before you select Cancel remain saved.

## File Links

### Purpose

Lists the supporting documents of the active linked document and enables you to open any supporting document. You also can switch links to a different document.

### To open linked documents

1. Activate the linked document you want to use.

2. Press Alt, F, L, or click the File menu and select Links.

   The names of all linked documents appear in the Links list box. Scroll through the list by pressing ↑, ↓, ←, →, PgDn, or PgUp, or by using the scroll bar.

3. Select the file(s) you want to open. To select adjoining files, press Shift+↑ or Shift+↓. To select nonadjoining files, press Ctrl+↑ or Ctrl+↓ to move through the list; press the space bar to select the files.

4. Turn on the Read Only option when you want to see the files but not change them.

5. To open the selected file(s), press Enter or click Open.

### To switch a link to a different document

1. Activate the linked document you want to use.

2. Press Alt, F, L, or click the File menu and select the Links command.

3. Select the supporting document you want to change and then select Change. A second dialog box appears.

4. Select the file from the list or type the name in the Copy from file text box, and then press Enter or click OK.

# File New

## *Purpose*

Creates a new worksheet, chart, or macro sheet in a window. The number of open documents is limited only by your system's memory.

## *To create a new file*

1. Press Alt, F, N, or click the File menu and select New.

   Excel asks whether you want to create a Worksheet, Chart, Macro Sheet, Workbook, or Slides.

2. Select the type of document you want to create, and then press Enter or click OK. The document appears in a new window and is selected.

## *Note*

Pressing Alt+Shift+F1 or Shift+F11 opens a new worksheet, Alt+F1 or F11 opens a new chart, and Alt+Ctrl+F1 or Ctrl+F11 opens a new macro sheet.

# File Open

## *Purpose*

Opens an existing file.

## *To open a file*

1. Press **Alt**, **F**, **O**; **Alt+Ctrl+F2**; or **Ctrl+F12**. You also can click the **F**ile menu and select **O**pen.

   Files in the current directory appear in the **F**iles list box. Available directories appear in the **D**irectories list box. Available drives appear in the Dri**v**es list box.

   Scroll through the **F**iles list using the scroll bar.

   Turn on the **R**ead Only check box if you want to see the file but not change it. (This option is applicable to networks, where several people may use the same file simultaneously.)

2. Select the file from the list of files or type its name in the File **N**ame box.

3. Press **Enter** or click **OK**.

## *Note*

In addition to its own Normal format, Excel can open files in the following formats:

| Format | Function |
|--------|----------|
| CSV | Comma Separated Values. |
| SYLK | Used by other Microsoft worksheets. |
| *.WK* | Used by Lotus 1-2-3 files. |
| DIF | Data Interchange Format. |
| *.DBF | Used by dBASE files. |
| Text | Also called ASCII, a generic PC format. Set text file options by selecting the Te**x**t button. |

## File Page Setup

### Purpose

Controls the appearance of the individual document, including margins, centering, headers, footers, orientation, and size. These settings link to the active document and save to disk. Use this command before printing with the File Print command.

### To set the appearance of a file

1. Activate the document whose print settings you want to adjust.

2. Press Alt, F, T, or click the File menu and select Page Setup.

3. Select the Portrait or Landscape orientation. The Portrait option prints the document down the length of the paper. The Landscape option prints the document across the width of the paper. These options will be dimmed if your printer cannot print.

4. Choose letter, legal, or other paper size from the Paper Size drop-down list.

5. Change the Left, Right, Top, and Bottom margins (in inches). Use decimal fractions if needed.

   Turn on Center Horizontally and Center Vertically to print the document centered between the margins.

6. Turn on Row & Column Headings to print the row numbers and column letters on each page.

   Turn on Cell Gridlines to print horizontal and vertical lines along the rows and columns on each page.

Turn on Black & White Cells to remove the patterns and color formats in cells for printing.

Type a number in the Start Page No.'s At box to start page numbering at a number other than 1.

7. To print pages from top to bottom and then right, select the Down then Over option button under Page Order. To print pages from left to right and then down, select the Over then Down option button. These two options are available only for sheets.

8. Select the Reduce/Enlarge To option button to specify the percentage of reduction or enlargement for a document. Select the Fit To option button to compress the document or selection during the printing process so that it can be printed on the specified page layout.

9. For charts, select the Size On Screen option button to print the chart the same size as it appears on-screen. Select the Scale to Fit Page option button to print the chart as large as possible while retaining the chart's height-to-width ratio as shown on the screen. Select the Use Full Page option button to print the chart to fit the page, adjusting the height-to-width ratio as necessary.

10. Select the Header or Footer button to display the Header or Footer dialog box, in which you can specify text, page numbers, and formatting for headers and footers.

    Default header and footer margins are always 0.5 inches from the top or bottom of the page and 0.75 inches from the side of the page.

11. Select the Printer Setup button to change certain default printer settings or to install printers.

Select the Printer you want to use.

Select Setup for more options. The options displayed depend on the printer you select.

Make appropriate changes, and then press Enter or click OK to save the settings and return to the first dialog box.

12. Press Enter or click OK. Your settings link with the document and are saved.

## Notes

When you work with a workgroup, any changes you make in the Page Setup dialog box change the settings for all documents in the workgroup.

If a chart embedded in a worksheet is selected, the specifications in the Page Setup dialog box refer only to the chart.

## File Print

## Purpose

Prints the active document.

## To print a file

1. Activate the document you want to print.

2. Prepare worksheets for printing by using the Options Set Print Area and Options Set Print Titles commands.

   Use the File Page Setup commands to adjust your printer options.

3. Press Alt, F, P; Alt+Ctrl+Shift+F2; or Ctrl+Shift+F12. You also can click the File menu and select Print.

4. Choose between printing All pages or selected pages. If you print selected pages, enter the page span in the From and To boxes.

5. Select the Print Quality from the drop-down list. This setting is dependent on the default printer.

6. Enter the number of Copies you want to print (the default is one copy). Depending on your printer, you also can collate multiple copies.

7. Choose to print only the Sheet values, only the cell Notes, or Both the values and the notes.

8. Choose Page Setup to get the Page Setup dialog box. This option is the same as File Page Setup command.

9. Turn on Preview and press Enter or click OK to see how the printed document will look— including page breaks—before you print. See also *File Print Preview*.

10. Click the Fast but no Graphics check box to print more quickly but exclude any graphs or graph objects inserted into the spreadsheet.

11. Press Enter or click OK to print.

## File Print Preview

### *Purpose*

Displays each page as it will look when printed.

### *To preview the printed page*

1. Activate the document you want to preview.

2. Press Alt, F, V, or click the File menu and select Preview.

3. Choose one of the following options:

   Next displays the next page of the document.

   Previous displays the previous page of the document.

   Zoom switches between full page view and actual size view.

   Print displays the File Print dialog box.

   Setup displays the File Page Setup dialog box.

   Margins enables you to adjust margins and column widths by dragging the markers.

   Close closes the Print Preview window and displays the active document.

## File Record Macro

### Purpose

Records your Excel actions in a macro file. This command duplicates the Macro Record command and is useful when all your files are closed, because only the File and Help menus are available.

### To record a macro

1. Plan the macro you want to record.

2. Press Alt, F, C, or click the File menu and select Record Macro.

3. Accept the suggested macro name (Record followed by a number) or type a different name.

4. Accept the suggested macro letter or type a different letter. (You run the macro by holding down **Ctrl** and pressing the macro letter you assigned it or by using the **Macro Run** command.)

5. Select to save the macro to the **Global Macro** Sheet or to a New **Macro** Sheet.

6. When you are ready to record your macro, press **Enter** or click **OK**.

7. If you chose to save the macro to a **Global** Macro Sheet, perform the actions you want to record.

   If you chose to save the macro to a New **Macro** Sheet, Excel opens a new macro sheet and starts recording in cell A1.

8. When you finish, press **Alt**, **F**, **C**, or click the **File** menu and select Stop Recorder. Alternatively, if you chose to save the macro to a New **Macro** Sheet, press **Alt**, **M**, **C**, or click the **Macro** menu and select Stop Recorder.

9. Save the macro sheet before you exit Excel.

## File Save

### *Purpose*

Saves a file to disk as you continue to work. If you have already named the file, your changes are saved immediately. If you have not named the file, the **File** Save **As** dialog box appears, enabling you to name the file.

> **CAUTION:** Save about every 15 minutes so that if your power source fails, you lose no more than 15 minutes of work.

### To save a file

Press Alt, F, S; Alt+Shift+F2; or Shift+F12. You also can click the File menu and select Save.

## File Save As

### Purpose

Saves a file to disk. Always displays a dialog box offering save options. Enables you to duplicate an existing document by saving it to a different file name.

### To save a file

1. Press Alt, F, A; Alt+F2; or F12. You also can click the File menu and select Save As. A dialog box appears.

2. To save under the suggested drive, directory, and file name, press Enter or click OK.

   To save under a different drive, select a drive from the Drives drop-down list.

   To save under a different directory, select a directory from the Directories list.

   To save under a different file name, type the name you want in the File Name box.

   Press Enter or click OK.

3. Select Options to set passwords and create backup files.

   Turn on Create Backup File to save the preceding version of your file on disk by renaming the file with the extension BAK.

Protect the file by assigning a Protection Password. The password can be up to 15 characters and can be made up of letters, numbers,
and symbols.

Enter a Write Reservation Password to require
a password to save changes to the file. This
option creates a read-only file unless you know
the password.

Select Read-Only Recommended to display a
message requesting that readers access the
file as a read-only file.

4. Press Enter or click OK. If you set passwords,
   you are prompted to verify them.

   Excel saves the file according to your settings.

### Note

Excel offers many file formats in which to save a file.
Select a file format from the Save File as Type drop-
down list.

## File Save Workbook

### Purpose

Saves the multiple files to a workbook file with the
extension XLW. When you open a workbook file, all
the files in that workbook open.

### To save a workbook

1. Press Alt, F, W, or click the File menu and
   select Save Workbook.

   A screen shows the current open documents
   that you can include in the workbook.

When you save a new workbook, the Save Workbook command displays the File Save As dialog box.

2. To accept the suggested name, press Enter or click OK. To use a different file name, type the name and then press Enter or click OK.

All open documents are saved individually, and the workbook information is saved in the new file you select.

### Notes

A workbook file does not contain the documents that were open when you created the file; it contains a list of those documents.

If you close a workbook file, Excel prompts you to save the changes you made to any of the individual files.

***Fig. 1.*** *Workbook icons.*

When you open a workbook, three icons appear in the rightmost corner of the horizontal scroll bar. Click the first icon to display a list of all the documents in the workbook. (To activate another workbook document, select a document from this list.) Click the second and third icons to scroll forward and backward, respectively, through the documents in the workbook.

## File Unhide

### Purpose

Lists hidden files when all files are closed. Makes the file you select visible.

### To display a hidden file

1. Press Alt, F, U, or click the File menu and select Unhide. A list of hidden files appears.

2. Select the file you want to see and press Enter or click OK.

### To hide an open window

Select the Window Hide command.

### Notes

If a file is open and another file is hidden, the Unhide command is in the Window menu. The Unhide command is dimmed if no files are hidden.

If a document is password-protected with the Options Protect Document command, Excel asks for a password before hiding or revealing the window.

# Format 3-D View

### Purpose

Controls the angle at which you view the data in a three-dimensional chart.

### To set the view angle for a 3-D chart

1. Press Alt, T, 3, or click the Format menu and select 3-D View. You also can click the right mouse button to bring up the shortcut menu and select 3-D View. This command is available only if the active chart is a 3-D chart.

2. Make the changes you want using the Elevation, Rotation, and Right Angle Axes choices. Choose either Auto Scaling or Height as a % of base.

3. Select Apply to change the current settings in the active chart without closing the dialog box.

   Select Default to retrieve the original chart settings.

4. Press Enter or click OK.

   Select Close or press Esc to cancel the 3-D View dialog box without making any changes to the chart.

___

**Note**

If you change the chart type using the Gallery menu, the 3-D View formats are not reset to their original values.

___

# Format Alignment

___

*Purpose*

Sets the alignment of selected cells.

___

*To set cell alignment*

1. Select the cells you want to align. (To select the entire worksheet, press Ctrl+Shift+space bar.)

2. Press Alt, T, A, or click the Format menu and select Alignment. You also can click the right mouse button to bring up the shortcut menu and select Alignment.

3. Select one of the following options:

   General                  Aligns text left, numbers right, and logical values and errors centered. (General is the default alignment.)

| | |
|---|---|
| Left, Center, or Right | Aligns all types of cell contents left, centered, or right, respectively. |
| Fill | Repeats the contents of the cell until the display is full (for example, 123 in a cell width of 9 displays as 123123123, but the actual value of 123 remains unaffected). |
| Justify | Aligns text within a cell to the right and left. This option is available only when the Wrap Text check box is selected. |
| Center across selection | Centers a cell entry across the selected cells. |

4. Select the Wrap Text check box if you want text to wrap according to the column width, increasing the row height accordingly.

5. Select to align cell entries with the Top, Center, or Bottom of a cell. The default is alignment to the bottom of the cell.

6. Select an Orientation for the selected cell entries. Selected cells' contents rotate according to the box you select. You must adjust the height of the row to the length of the rotated text.

7. Press Enter or click OK.

---

*Note*

Blank cells that are part of a Fill range take on the display of the cells to their left. You can use this feature to create a border with a character or mix of characters.

## Format AutoFormat

### Purpose

Enables you to apply a built-in format automatically to a range of cells or a table on a worksheet.

### To autoformat a range or a table

1. Select the range or table.

2. Press Alt, T, M, or click the Format menu and select AutoFormat.

3. Select the format you want to apply from the Table Format list. The Sample box displays an example of the selected format.

4. Select Options to apply specific formats. The default applies Number, Border, Font, Patterns, Alignment, and Width/Height.

## Format Border

### Purpose

Adds lines, boxes, and shading to selected cells.

### To format borders

1. Select the cells you want to format with a border. (To select the entire worksheet, press Ctrl+Shift+space bar.)

2. Press Alt, T, B, or click the Format menu and select Border. You also can click the right mouse button to bring up the shortcut menu and select Border.

3. Select one or more of the following options:

| | |
|---|---|
| Outline | Draws a rectangular box around the range of cells. |
| Left | Draws a line to the left of each cell. |
| Right | Draws a line to the right of each cell. |
| Top | Draws a line above each cell. |
| Bottom | Draws a line below each cell. |

4. Select Style and Color options. Select the Shade box if you want a shaded border.

5. Press Enter or click OK.

## Format Bring To Front

### Purpose

Places the selected object in front of all other objects.

### To bring an object to the front

1. Select the object in the background that you want to bring to the foreground. (This command has no effect if the selected object is already in front.)

2. Press Alt, T, O, or click the Format menu and select Bring To Front. You also can click the right mouse button to bring up the shortcut menu and select Bring to Front.

## Format Cell Protection

### Purpose

Safeguards selected cells and their formulas. Options Protect Document must be off.

### To protect selected cells

1. Select the cells you want to protect. (To select the entire worksheet, press **Ctrl+Shift+space bar**.)

2. Press **Alt**, **T**, **I**, or click the Format menu and select Cell Protection.

3. Turn on the Locked option to prevent editing of the cell contents.

4. Turn on the Hidden option to prevent the formulas from appearing in the formula bar and Info window.

5. Press **Enter** or click **OK**.

6. Select the Options Protect Document command and turn on Cells.

## Format Column Width

### Purpose

Sets the display width of selected columns, without affecting the amount of data the columns can hold.

## *To set a column width*

1. Select at least one cell from each of the columns you want to change. (To change the width of all columns in the worksheet, select one entire row by pressing **Shift+space bar**.)

2. Press **Alt**, **T**, **C**, or click the Format menu and select Column Width.

3. To specify a new column width, type a number from 0 to 255, indicating the number of characters you want in a cell. Your number can include decimal fractions, which represent fractions of a character.

4. Turn on the Standard Width option to reset the columns. The standard width is determined by the number in the Standard Width box (8.43 characters by default).

5. Select Hide to set the column width to zero and remove the column from view.

   If a column is hidden, select the column headings on both sides of the hidden column and select the Unhide command to display the hidden column.

6. Select Best Fit if you want the column width to adjust to the widest cell in the column. You also can double-click the right border of the column heading.

7. Set the standard width for columns in the Standard Width box.

8. Press **Enter** or click **OK**.

## *To set column width with the mouse*

Click and drag the right border of the column heading.

### Notes

If a column is too narrow to display the contents of a formatted cell, multiple pound signs (####) appear in that cell. If a column is too narrow to display the contents of an unformatted cell, the number appears in exponential format.

To change the column widths in several worksheets at once, use the Options Group Edit command.

## Format Font

### Purpose

Changes the font, style, size, and color for selected cells, chart text, or the entire document.

### To change the font

1. Select the cells or chart text whose fonts you want to change.

2. Press Alt, T, F, or click the Format menu and select Font. You also can click the right mouse button to bring up the shortcut menu and select Font.

3. Select the Font, Font Style, Size, and Color choices from the dialog box. A sample of your choices appears in the sample area.

4. In the Effects area of the dialog box, turn on Strikeout to place a line through the selected text.

   Turn on Underline to underline the selected text.

5. In a worksheet or macro sheet, select the Normal Font box to set the font, font style, size, and effects to be the normal style.

6. In a chart, select a background of Automatic to apply the default background, Transparent to leave the area behind the text transparent, or Opaque to remove any pattern but leave the foreground color behind the text.

7. Press Enter or click OK.

## Format Group (Ungroup)

### Purpose

Creates a single graphic object from several selected graphic objects, or ungroups a group of objects. This command is available only when the active document is a worksheet or macro sheet.

### To group or ungroup objects

1. Select the objects you want to group. Use the selection tool on the Toolbar to select the objects you want to group, or hold down the Shift key as you select each object.

   The Format Group command is dimmed when only one object is selected.

2. Press Alt, T, G, or click the Format menu and select Group. (Ungroup is displayed when a grouped object is selected.)

   The selected objects are now grouped as a single object, and you can move, size, and format them as one object. (The Format Ungroup command ungroups the objects, making each one separate.)

## Format Justify

### Purpose

Changes column text into a word-wrapped paragraph.

### To justify column text

1. Select a range of cells that contains text as the leftmost column and blank cells in the rest of the range.

2. Press **Alt**, **T**, **J**, or click the Format menu and select **Justify**.

   To the extent permitted by the width of the range, the text in the range's lower rows moves to combine with the text in the upper rows. If the range is not large enough for the justification, a warning box appears on-screen. Press **Enter** or click **OK** to continue the justification beyond the selected range, or choose Cancel to stop the operation.

   Blank cells in the text column act as separators, creating multiple paragraphs. (The cells must be blank, not just cells containing spaces.)

## Format Legend

### Purpose

Changes the position of the active chart's legend.

### *To move the legend with the keyboard*

1. Select the legend.

2. Press Alt, T, L, or click the Format menu and select Legend.

3. Select the position of the legend at the chart's Bottom, top right Corner, Top, Right, or Left. The default position is Right.

4. To accept your settings and return to the chart, press Enter or click OK.

   To accept your settings and move on to another chart Format command, select Patterns or Font.

### *To move the legend with the mouse*

Click and drag the legend to any position on the chart.

## Format Main Chart

### *Purpose*

Sets type and formatting of the active main chart, and enables you to change chart types without losing custom formatting.

### *To format a main chart*

1. Press Alt, T, M, or click the Format menu and select Main Chart. You also can click the right mouse button to bring up the shortcut menu and select Main Chart.

2. Select one of 13 Chart Types: Area, Bar, Column, Line, Pie, XY (Scatter), Radar, 3-D Area, 3-D Bar, 3-D Column, 3-D Line, 3-D Pie, or 3-D Surface.

3. Choose from the available options, which vary according to the chart type.

| | |
|---|---|
| Data View | Shows available marker arrangements for the selected chart type. |
| Overlap | Determines overlap of markers in a bar or column chart. |
| Gap Width | Determines space between clusters in a bar or column chart. |
| Series Lines | Connects the tops of the data markers for each series in a stacked bar or stacked column chart. |
| Vary by Category | Gives each data point in a single series a different color. |
| Drop Lines | Extends lines from the highest value in each category to the category axis. |
| Hi-Lo Lines | Extends lines from the highest to lowest value in each category so that you can create an open-high-low-close chart (if you selected the Line chart type). |
| Up/Down Bars | Creates an up/down bar extending from the opening price to the closing price so that you can create an open-high-low-close chart (if you selected the Line chart type). |

| | |
|---|---|
| Radar Axis Labels | Displays labels for category axes on radar charts. |
| Angle of First Pie Slice (degrees) | Sets the angle of the first edge of the first slice in a pie chart. |
| 3-D Gap Depth | Sets distance between data series in a 3-D chart. |
| 3-D Chart Depth | Sets depth of 3-D chart relative to its width. |

The default is a Column chart with all other options turned off and Gap Width set at 50 percent.

4. Press Enter or click OK.

## Format Move

### *Purpose*

Enables you to move the active chart's objects.

### *To move a chart object*

1. Select the chart object you want to move.

2. Press Alt, T, V, or click the Format menu and select Move.

3. Press ↑, ↓, ←, or → to position the object. To move in smaller increments, hold down Ctrl and press ↑, ↓, ←, or →.

   With the mouse, click and drag the object.

4. When the object is in the desired location, press Enter.

# Format Number

## *Purpose*

Sets the number, date, or time format of the values in selected cells.

## *To format numbers*

1. Select the cells whose numeric, date, or time values you want to format. (To select the entire worksheet, press Ctrl+Shift+space bar.)

2. Press Alt, T, N, or click the Format menu and select Number. You also can click the right mouse button to bring up the shortcut menu and select Number.

3. Select a format from the Format Codes list, which contains a list of 27 different formats, including integers, scientific notation, currency, percentages, dates, and times. The default format is General.

4. Press Enter or click OK.

## *Note*

You can create a custom number format by customizing a built-in format or typing a new format in the Code box. After you press Enter or click OK, the custom formats appear with the built-in formats in the Format Codes list.

# Format Object Properties

## *Purpose*

Controls how graphic objects are attached to cells.

## *To move a graphic object*

1. Select the object you want to move.

2. Press **Alt**, **T**, **E**, or click the Format menu and select the Object Properties command. You also can click the right mouse button to bring up the shortcut menu and select Object Properties.

3. Select the button that describes how you want the object to move and size:

   Move and Size with Cells sets an object to change its position and size with the cells under its upper-left and lower-right corners.

   Move but Don't Size with Cells sets an object to move with the cells under its upper-left corner, but does not change the size of the object. This is the default setting.

   Don't Move or Size with Cells sets an object to detach itself from the underlying cell grid so that it maintains its position and size, regardless of changes to the cells.

   Turn on Print Object if you want the object to print with the worksheet.

# Format Object Protection

## *Purpose*

Protects the selected object or text box in a worksheet or macro sheet from being moved or modified. This command is available only when an object or text box is selected and the Options Protect Document command has not been executed.

## *To protect an object*

1. Select the object you want to protect.

2. Press Alt, T, I, or click the Format menu and select the Object Protection command.

   To prevent the selected object from being protected when the document is protected, turn off the Locked check box.

   If your object contains text, you can prevent text in a selected text box from being edited when the document is protected by turning on the Lock Text box. You can move or size the text box, but you cannot edit or format the text within the text box.

3. Press Enter or click OK.

4. Select the Options Protect Document command and turn on Objects.

# Format Overlay

## *Purpose*

Sets the type and formatting of the active overlay chart.

### To format an overlay chart

1. Activate a chart with an overlay.

2. Press Alt, T, O, or click the Format menu and select the Overlay command. You also can click the right mouse button to bring up the shortcut menu and select Overlay.

3. Select from the options in the Format Overlay Chart dialog box. (See *Format Main Chart* for an explanation of these options.)

4. Press Enter or click OK.

## Format Patterns

### Purpose

Sets the style, color, weight, and pattern of the selected objects. Sets the cell shading for selected cells in a worksheet or macro sheet.

### To apply formats to an object in a worksheet or macro sheet

1. Select the object you want to format.

2. Press Alt, T, P, or click the Format menu and select the Patterns command. You also can click the right mouse button to bring up the shortcut menu and select Patterns.

   The pattern options vary according to the object you selected.

3. Choose from the available Border options:

   | | |
   |---|---|
   | Automatic | Applies the default border pattern. |
   | None | Displays the object without a border. |

| Style | Sets the style of the object's border. |
|---|---|
| Color | Sets the color of the object's border. |
| Weight | Sets the weight of the object's border. |
| Round Corners | Rounds the corners of the object's border. |

4. Choose from the available Fill options:

| Automatic | Applies the default fill pattern. |
|---|---|
| None | Displays the object without fill. |
| Pattern | Sets the pattern of the fill. |
| Foreground | Sets the foreground color of the fill. |
| Background | Sets the background color of the fill. |

5. To accept your settings and return to the worksheet, press **Enter** or click **OK**.

### To apply formats to an item in a chart

1. Select the chart item you want to format.

2. Press **Alt**, **T**, **P**, or click the Format menu and select the **P**atterns command. You also can click the right mouse button to bring up the shortcut menu and select Patterns.

   The pattern options vary according to the item you selected.

3. Choose from the available Border options:

| Automatic | Applies the default item pattern. |
|---|---|
| None | Displays the item without a border. |

| Style | Sets the style of the item's border. |
| Color | Sets the color of the item's border. |
| Weight | Sets the weight of the item's border. |
| Shadow | Creates a shadow for the item's border. |

4. Choose from the available Area options:

| Automatic | Applies the default area pattern. |
| None | Displays the area without fill. |
| Pattern | Sets the pattern of the item. |
| Foreground | Sets the foreground item. |
| Background | Sets the background item. |

5. When applicable, choose from the available Arrowhead options:

| Style | Sets the style of the arrowhead. |
| Width | Sets the width of the arrowhead. |
| Length | Sets the length of the arrowhead. |

6. To accept your settings and return to the chart, press Enter or click OK.

---

### *To apply cell shading*

1. Select a pattern from the Pattern drop-down list box. The default is None.

2. Select a color from the Foreground drop-down list box. The default is Automatic.

3. Select a color from the **B**ackground drop-down list box. The default is Automatic.

4. Press **Enter** or click **OK**.

# Format Row Height

### *Purpose*

Sets the height of selected rows.

### *To set row height with the keyboard*

1. Select at least one cell from each of the rows whose height you want to change. (To change the height of all rows in the worksheet, select one entire column by pressing **Ctrl+space bar**.)

2. Press **Alt**, **T**, **R**, or click the Format menu and select **R**ow Height.

3. To specify a new row height, type the height's point size (72 points = 1 inch), which can range from 0 (which hides the rows from view) to 409. Your number can include decimal fractions, which represent fractions of a point.

   Turn on **S**tandard Height (12.75 points) to reset the rows.

   Select **Hi**de to set the row height to zero and remove the row from view. To display a hidden row, select the row headings on both sides of the hidden row and select the **U**nhide command.

   To change the column widths in several worksheets at once, use the **O**ptions **G**roup Edit command.

4. Press **Enter** or click **OK**.

### *To set row height with the mouse*

Click and drag the bottom border of the row's heading.

## Format Scale

### *Purpose*

Controls the scale setting for each axis on the active chart.

### *To set the scale of an axis*

1. Select either the category (X) axis, value (Y) axis, or data series axis (the y-axis on a 3-D chart).

2. Press **Alt**, **T**, **S**, or click the Format menu and select **S**cale.

   Different options are available, depending on the chart type and axis you are formatting.

3. Select from the following available options:

   **Category (X) Axis Scale Options**

   Value (Y) Axis **C**rosses at Category Number, which specifies the number of the category where the value (Y) axis crosses the category (X) axis (usually 1).

   Number of Categories Between Tick **L**abels.

   Number of Categories Between Tick Mar**k**s.

   Value (Y) Axis Crosses **B**etween Categories.

   Categories in **R**everse Order, which displays categories from right to left.

   Value (Y) Axis Crosses at **M**aximum Category, which makes the value (Y) axis cross the category (X) axis at the last category.

   The **P**atterns, **F**ont, and **T**ext buttons, which enable you to apply formatting to those elements.

### Value (Y) Axis Scale Options

Minimum and Maximum values the chart will display.

Major Unit and Minor Unit for the distance between major and minor tick marks.

Category (X) Axis Crosses At, which specifies where the category (X) axis crosses the value (Y) axis.

Whether Logarithmic Scale is used to calculate the preceding setting.

Values in Reverse Order, which displays values in descending order.

Category (X) Axis Crosses at Maximum Value, which makes the category (X) axis cross the value (Y) axis at the highest value.

The Patterns, Font, and Text buttons, which enable you to apply formatting to those elements.

### Data Series Axis Scale Options

Number of Series Between Tick Labels.

Number of Series Between Tick Marks.

Series in Reverse Order, which reverses order of the series.

The Patterns, Font, and Text buttons, which enable you to apply formatting to those elements.

4. To accept your setting and return to the chart, press Enter or click OK.

# Format Send to Back

## *Purpose*

Places the selected object behind all other objects.

### To send an object to the back

1. Select the object in the foreground that you want to place in the background. (This command has no effect if the selected object is already in the background.)

2. Press Alt, T, K, or click the Format menu and select Send to Back. You also can click the right mouse button to bring up the shortcut menu and select Send to Back.

## Format Size

### Purpose

Enables you to resize chart arrows and detached text boxes in a chart.

### To resize a chart object with the keyboard

1. Select the chart object.

2. Press Alt, T, Z, or click the Format menu and select Size.

3. Press ↑, ↓, ←, or → to resize the object in either or both dimensions. To resize in smaller increments, hold down Ctrl and press ↑, ↓, ←, or →.

4. When the object is the correct size, press Enter.

### To resize a chart object with the mouse

Click and drag the object's black selection squares.

## Format Style

### Purpose

Defines a cell style based on the selected formats and assigns the style a name.

### To create a style by example

1. Select a cell that has the desired combination of formats.

2. Press Alt, T, S, or click the Format menu and select Style.

3. Select a style name from the Style Name drop-down list, or type a new name.

4. Press Enter or click OK.

### To create a style by definition

1. Press Alt, T, S, or click the Format menu and select Style.

2. Type a name for the style in the Style dialog box.

3. Select Define. The Style dialog box expands to display six cell attributes.

4. Turn on the check boxes for the cell attributes you want to include in the style.

5. Under Change, select the button for the attribute you want to add or change.

6. Select the formats you want to use for the selected text by clicking the appropriate choice.

7. Press Enter or click OK to confirm your choices and close the Style dialog box.

## Format Text

### Purpose

Sets the alignment and orientation of text in a chart or in a worksheet text box.

### To format text

1. Select the text in the chart or worksheet text box that you want to format.

2. Press Alt, T, T, or click the Format menu and select Text.

3. Select horizontal or vertical alignment options. Select Orientation.

   In a chart, you also specify the following options:

   Turn on Automatic Text

   Turn on Automatic Size

   Show Key to

4. Press Enter or click OK to accept your settings.

## Formula Apply Names

### Purpose

Replaces formula cell references with designated names.

### To apply names

1. Select a cell or range whose formula cell references you want to replace with created or defined names.

2. Press **Alt, R, A** or click the Formula menu and select **A**pply Names.

   All existing names in the active worksheet appear in the Apply Names list box.

3. Press ↑ or ↓ to highlight the name you want to apply. Then press the **space bar** or click to select or deselect a name.

4. Choose from the following options:

   **I**gnore Relative/Absolute replaces references regardless of their types.

   **U**se Row and Column Names applies names to references that are not exact matches.

   If you then select **O**ptions, you can set whether to Omit **C**olumn Name if Same Column, Omit **R**ow Name if Same Row, or display a cell reference replaced by row-oriented and column-oriented names in Ro**w** Column or Co**l**umn Row order.

5. Press **Enter** or click **OK**.

### Note

See also *Formula Create Names* and *Formula Define Name*.

# Formula Create Names

### *Purpose*

Names cells within a range using the text at specified edges of the range.

### *To create names*

1. Enter the names you want to create in the
   specified location: the top row, left column,
   bottom row, or right column of the range.
   Names must begin with a letter.

2. Select the range.

3. Press **Alt, R, C**; press **Ctrl+Shift+F3**; or click
   the Formula menu and select Create Names.

4. Select the check boxes indicating the location
   of the names you want to create.

5. Press **Enter** or click **OK**.

### *Note*

See also *Formula Apply Names* and *Formula Define
Name*.

# Formula Define Name

### *Purpose*

Names a cell range, value, or formula. Enables you
to edit and delete existing names.

### To name a range, value, or formula

1. Select the range, value, or formula you want to name.

2. Press **Alt, R, D**; press **Ctrl+F3**; or click the Formula menu and select **D**efine Name.

3. If you selected a range, name the selected range. Names must begin with a letter and cannot include spaces.

4. After defining names, press **Enter** or click **OK**.

### To revise an existing name or reference

1. Select the range.

2. Press **Alt, R, D**; press **Ctrl+F3**; or click the Formula menu and select **D**efine Name.

3. Edit the name or reference.

4. Press **Enter** or click **OK**.

### To delete a name from the Names in Sheet list

1. Press **Alt, R, D**; press **Ctrl+F3**; or click the Formula menu and select **D**efine Name.

2. Select the name from the Names in **S**heet list.

3. Select **D**elete.

   Delete names with caution. You cannot undo the deletion of a name.

4. Press **Enter** or click **OK**.

### Note

See also *Formula Apply Names* and *Formula Create Names*.

## Formula Find

### *Purpose*

Finds the next occurrence of the specified text or number.

### *To find a specified text or number*

1. Select the range whose contents you want to search. If you do not select a range, Excel searches the entire worksheet.

2. Press Alt, R, F; press Shift+F5; or click the Formula menu and select Find.

3. Type the text or number you want to find in the Find What box. You can include the DOS wild cards.

4. Select whether to look in Formulas, Values, or Notes.

5. Select Whole to find occurrences that are an entire cell, or select Part to find occurrences that are part of longer text or number sequences.

6. Select whether to search by Rows or Columns.

7. Turn on Match Case for case sensitivity.

8. Press Enter or click OK.

9. To find the next occurrence, press F7. To find the preceding occurrence, press Shift+F7.

10. Repeat step 9 to find all occurrences.

### *Note*

See also *Formula Replace*.

## Formula Goal Seek

### Purpose

Varies the value in a specified cell until a formula dependent on that cell reaches the desired value.

### To solve for a desired result

1. Select the cell containing the formula for which you want to find a specific solution.

2. Press **Alt**, **R**, **L** or click the Formula menu and select Goal Seek.

3. Enter the value you want the formula to produce in the To value box.

4. In the By changing cell box, enter the cell reference or select the cell containing the value (not a formula) that you want Excel to change to produce the specified result.

5. Press **Enter** or click **OK**. You can pause or stop the calculation by selecting the Pause or Cancel button.

6. To replace the old value with the value found with the Goal Seek command, press **Enter** or click **OK**. Press **Esc** or click Cancel to keep the old value.

## Formula Goto

### Purpose

Locates and selects the specified cell or named range.

### To go to a named range

1. Press Alt, R, G; press F5; or click the Formula menu and select Goto.

2. Select a name from the Goto list or type a name or a cell address in the Reference box.

3. Press Enter or click OK.

## Formula Note

### Purpose

Enables you to add, view, edit, and delete notes in a cell.

### To add or edit a note

1. Select the cell in which you want to add or edit a note.

2. Press Alt, R, N; press Shift+F2; or click the Formula menu and select Note.

3. Add text or edit the existing text in the Text Note dialog box. To delete a note, select the note from the Notes in Sheet box, click Delete, and then press Enter or click OK.

4. Press Enter or click OK to accept the changes and close the dialog box. Select Add to accept the changes and keep the dialog box open.

## Formula Outline

### Purpose

Creates an outline from an existing worksheet or range.

### To create an outline

1. Select the range you want to outline. If you select a single cell, Excel outlines the entire worksheet.

2. Press **Alt**, **R**, **O**; or click the Formula menu and select Outline.

3. Turn on the Automatic Styles check box if you want Excel to apply built-in outline styles to rows and columns. Select the check boxes to specify the direction you want the levels to flow in the outline.

4. Select Create.

# Formula Paste Function

### Purpose

Lists all predefined Excel worksheet formulas, and inserts the selected formula and (optionally) its arguments in the formula bar.

### To paste a function into a cell

1. Select the cell in which you want to paste the formula.

2. Press **Alt**, **R**, **T**; press **Shift**+**F3**; or click the Formula menu and select Paste Function.

3. Select the Function Category or leave All selected.

4. Select the name of the function you want to insert from the Paste Function list (jump to a function by pressing its first letter).

5. To insert only the function name in the formula bar, press **Enter** or click **OK**. To include the arguments, turn on Paste Arguments and press **Enter** or click **OK**.

6. If you included the argument names, replace the argument placeholders with the appropriate arguments.

# Formula Paste Name

### Purpose

Lists all worksheet names and inserts the selected name in the formula bar.

> **CAUTION:** The List overwrites any existing worksheet data, so make sure that you position the cell selector correctly.

### To paste a name into a cell

1. Select the cell in which you want to build a formula using a defined name.

2. Press **Alt**, **R**, **P**; press **F3**; or click the Formula menu and select **P**aste Name.

3. Select the name you want (jump to a name by pressing its first letter).

4. To insert the selected name in the formula bar, press **Enter** or click **OK**. The name appears in the formula bar. Complete the formula and press **Enter**.

5. To insert a list of all defined names and their references in the worksheet starting at the active cell, select Paste List.

# Formula Replace

### *Purpose*

Searches for the specified text or number and replaces it with another text or number.

### *To replace a specified text or number*

1. Select the range whose contents you want to search and replace. If you do not select a range, Excel searches the entire worksheet.

2. Press **Alt, R, E** or click the Formula menu and select Replace.

3. Type the text or number you want to replace in the Find What box. You can include DOS wild cards.

4. Type the replacement text or number in the Replace With dialog box.

5. Select Whole or Part.

6. Select whether to search by Rows or Columns.

7. Turn on Match Case for case sensitivity.

8. To find the next occurrence, select Find Next. To find the preceding occurrence, press and hold **Shift** and select Find Next.

9. To replace the current occurrence and then find the next occurrence, select Replace. Continue this procedure to replace all further occurrences.

   When Excel finds no more matches, press **Enter** or click OK to clear the dialog box.

10. Select Replace All to replace all occurrences of the text. If you do not like the results, select Edit Undo Replace.

11. After making replacements, press **Esc** or click Close to close the Replace With dialog box.

### Note

See also *Formula Find*.

## Formula Select Special

### Purpose

Selects all cells that fit the specified description.

### To select cells

1. Select the range you want to search. If you do not select a range, Excel searches the entire worksheet.

2. Press **Alt**, **R**, **S** or click the Formula menu and select the Select Special command.

3. Choose whether to select cells containing Notes, Constants, Formulas (formula Numbers, Text, Logicals, or Errors), or Blanks.

   Or select Current Region, Current Array, Row Differences, or Column Differences.

   Or select Precedents or Dependents at the Direct Only level or at All Levels.

   Or select Last Cell, Visible Cells Only, or Objects.

4. Press **Enter** or click **OK**.

# Formula Show Active Cell

### Purpose

Scrolls the worksheet until the active cell is in view.

### To display the active cell

Press **Alt**, **R**, **H** or click the Formula menu and select Show Active Cell. This command is effective only if the active cell is not visible.

# Formula Solver

### Purpose

Solves for a specific solution based on defined parameters and constraints.

### To solve for a specified solution

1. Select the cell whose value you want to maximize, minimize, or reach a certain value.

2. Press **Alt**, **R**, **V** or click the Formula menu and select Solver.

3. Select the **Max**, **Min**, or **V**alue of: option. If the Value of: option is selected, enter the desired value in the box.

4. In the **B**y Changing Cells box, select the cell(s) to be adjusted by Solver.

5. Select cell(s) that are subject to constraints and specify the constraints. The **O**ptions button controls advanced features of the solution process.

6. Select **S**olve to initiate the problem-solving process for the defined problem. **R**eset All clears all settings from the dialog box. Close closes the dialog box without saving the settings.

## Gallery

### Purpose

Lists chart types and enables selection among several predefined formats for each chart type.

### To select a predefined chart format

1. Press **Alt**, **G** or click the **G**allery menu and select the chart type you want to use.

   Excel displays several predefined formats for that chart type. To see the formats for other chart types on the **G**allery menu, select **N**ext or **P**revious.

2. Double-click the chart format you want to use or select the chart and press **Enter** or click OK.

   Excel applies the format to the active chart. If the active chart has an overlay, the overlay is deleted.

## Gallery Preferred

### Purpose

Applies the format you defined with the **G**allery Set Preferred command to the active chart.

### To apply the preferred chart format

Press **Alt**, **G**, **R** or click the **G**allery menu and select Preferred.

## Gallery Set Preferred

### Purpose

Changes the default chart format to one you specify.

> **CAUTION:** The preferred format is lost when you exit Excel, unless you use the **F**ile Save **W**orkbook command to save the workbook.

### To set the preferred chart format

1. Create a chart that uses the chart type and formats you want to use as the default for all new charts.

2. Press **Alt**, **G**, **T** or click the **G**allery menu and select Set Preferred. Select the **G**allery Preferred command to apply your selected format to the active chart.

## Help Index

### Purpose

Displays a Help window of Excel topics.

### *To locate and display Excel Help topics*

1. Press Alt, H, C or click the Help menu and select Contents.

2. Select a Help topic from the list.

3. To close the Help window, press Alt, F, X; press Alt+F4; or click the File menu (in the Help window, not the document window) and select Exit.

### *To display Excel equivalents of Lotus 1-2-3 commands*

1. Press Alt, H, L or click the Help menu and select Lotus 1-2-3.

2. Choose the Instructions or Demo option. Select Faster or Slower buttons (1-5) to control the speed of the demonstration. Choose the More Help button for a list of topics for assistance.

3. Select the Lotus 1-2-3 command you want to perform.

### *To run the Help tutorial*

1. Press Alt, H, E or click the Help menu and select Learning Microsoft Excel.

2. Excel prompts you to press Enter or click Yes to save any open document(s).

3. Select the topic for which you want help.

4. To quit Help Learning Microsoft Excel, press X; click the Exit button (from the Main Menu); or press Ctrl+F1, X. You also can click the Controls button and then the Exit button (from the Program Control menu).

# Info

## Purpose

Displays information about active cells. Excel has eight Info commands that appear in the Info window.

## To display information about the active cell

1. Select the cell whose information you want to display.

2. Press Alt, O, W or click the Options menu, select Workspace, and select Info Window under Display.

3. To close the Info window, press Ctrl+F4; or click the Info window Control menu bar and select Close to close the Info window and return to the worksheet.

4. To keep the Info window available, press Alt, W and select another window. To go back to the Info window, simply choose it from under Window at any point.

# Macro Assign to Object

## Purpose

Assigns a macro to an object on a worksheet or macro sheet. The macro runs when you click the object.

### *To assign a macro to an object*

1. Open the macro sheet containing the macro you want to assign to the object.

2. Select the graphic object in which you want to attach the macro.

3. Press Alt, M, O or click the Macro menu and select Assign to Object.

4. Select the macro from the Assign Macro box, which displays all macros from the global macro sheet and any open macro sheet, or type the macro name in the Reference box.

5. If you do not select a macro from the Assign Macro box, you can choose Record to record your subsequent actions as a macro assigned to the object.

6. Press Enter or click OK.

## Macro Assign to Tool

### *Purpose*

Assigns a macro to a tool on a Toolbar. The macro runs when you click the tool. This command only appears on the Macro menu when you are customizing a Toolbar.

### *To assign a macro to a tool*

1. Press Alt, O, O or click the Options menu and select Toolbars.

2. Select the Toolbar to contain the tool assigned the macro, and then choose Show. The Toolbar will now display on-screen.

3. Press **Alt**, **O**, **O** or click the **O**ptions menu and select T**o**olbars.

4. Choose **C**ustomize.

5. On the Toolbar, select the tool to which you want to assign the macro.

6. Press **Alt**, **M**, **O** or click the **M**acro menu and select Assign to T**o**ol.

7. Select the macro from the Assign **M**acro box, which displays all macros from the global macro sheet and any open macro sheet, or type the macro name in the Re**f**erence box.

8. If you do not select a macro from the Assign **M**acro box, you can choose **R**ecord to record your subsequent actions as a macro assigned to the tool.

9. Press **Enter** or click **OK**.

## Macro Record

### *Purpose*

Records your Excel commands and keystrokes on a macro sheet. This command appears only when you are not recording a macro.

### *To record a macro*

1. Plan the macro you want to record.

2. Press **Alt**, **M**, **C** or click the **M**acro menu and select Re**c**ord.

3. Type a **N**ame for the macro or accept the default.

4. Type a shortcut **K**ey for the macro or accept the default.

5. Select to store the macro in either the Global Macro Sheet or a New Macro Sheet. If you already have other macro(s) stored on the same sheet, the option may say Macro Sheet followed by a name in parentheses, for example (Macro 2).

6. When you are ready to perform the actions, press Enter or click OK.

7. Perform the actions you want to record.

8. After performing the actions, press Alt, M, C again or click the Macro menu and select Stop Recorder.

   To view the macro sheet after the macro is recorded, press Alt, W and select the macro sheet.

9. To run the macro, press Ctrl plus the shortcut key, or select the Macro Run command and then select the macro name.

10. To save the macro, save its macro sheet with the File Save command.

# Macro Relative (Absolute) Record

### Purpose

Records macro cell references as absolute references, or records macro cell references as relative references.

### To record relative references

Press Alt, M, A or click the Macro menu and select Relative Record. This command is the default setting.

### *To record absolute references*

Press **Alt**, **M**, **A** or click the **M**acro menu and select **A**bsolute Record.

### *Notes*

With the **A**bsolute Record command, the macro operates on a fixed range of cells each time it is run. This command appears only when you select **M**acro Relative Record.

With the Relative Record command, the macro operates on cells a fixed distance from the active cell when run. This command appears only when you select **M**acro **A**bsolute Record.

You can select these commands before and during macro recording.

## Macro Resume

### *Purpose*

Continues a macro after a PAUSE macro function or after the Pause button in Single-Step mode has been chosen.

### *To resume a macro*

Press **Alt**, **M**, **E** or click the **M**acro menu and select Resume.

# Macro Run

## *Purpose*

Lists all named macros on open macro sheets and runs the macro you select.

## *To run a macro*

1. Press **Alt**, **M**, **R** or click the **M**acro menu and select **R**un.

2. Select the macro you want to run from the **R**un list or type the complete macro name (the macro sheet name, an exclamation point, and the name of the macro) in the Reference box.

   Select **S**tep if you want the macro to execute one step at a time. The **S**tep option brings up a dialog box that includes the following choices:

   **S**tep Into steps through the next macro instruction including user-defined function calls.

   Step **O**ver steps through the next macro instruction excluding user-defined function calls.

   **E**valuate evaluates each macro step.

   **P**ause pauses macro execution. Resume macro execution by choosing **M**acro Re-sume.

   **H**alt stops execution of the macro.

   **C**ontinue executes the remainder of the macro without stepping.

Goto stops the macro and activates the cell currently being evaluated.

3. Press **Enter** or click **OK**.

## Macro Set Recorder

### *Purpose*

Defines a range in a macro sheet for storing macros recorded with the **Macro Start Recorder** command.

### *To set a range on a macro sheet*

1. Activate the macro sheet that will store the macro.

2. Select the range in the macro sheet in which you want to record. If you select a single cell, the recording starts in that cell and continues downward in the same column.

3. Press **Alt**, **M**, **T** or click the **Macro** menu and select Set Recorder.

## Macro Start Recorder

### *Purpose*

Records your Excel actions on a macro sheet.

### *To record a macro*

1. Plan the macro you want to record.

2. Activate a new or existing macro sheet.

3. Select the range in the macro sheet in which you want to record the macro and select Macro Set Recorder.

4. Activate the document in which you want to perform your actions.

5. Press Alt, M, S or click the Macro menu and select Start Recorder.

6. Perform the actions you want to record.

   Excel records the actions in the range defined with the Set Recorder command.

7. Press Alt, M, C or click the Macro menu and select Stop Recorder.

8. To run the macro, select the Macro Run command.

9. To save the macro, use the File Save command.

# Macro Stop Recorder

## Purpose

Turns off the macro recording. You must be in Macro Record mode for this command to be available.

## To stop recording a macro

Press Alt, M, C or click the Macro menu and select Stop Recorder.

To resume recording, select Macro Start Recorder. The macro resumes recording at the point at which it was stopped.

# Options Calculation

## Purpose

Controls how Excel calculates formulas in worksheets and charts.

## To set calculation options

1. Press **Alt, O, C** or click the **O**ptions menu and select **C**alculation.

2. Select one of three calculation options:

   Automatic    Calculates all formulas that refer to a changed cell (the default setting).

   Automatic except Tables    Excepts tables because Excel calculates them more slowly.

   Manual    Prevents automatic calculation. The Recalculate Before Save check box is turned on when the manual calculation option is selected.

3. Select Iteration limits. Excel's defaults are 100 for Maximum Iterations and 0.001 for Maximum Change.

4. Turn on or off the following features:

   Update Remote References    Controls the calculation of formulas referring to other applications.

| | |
|---|---|
| Precision as Displayed | Speeds calculations but limits their accuracy. |
| 1904 Date System | Sets how Excel calculates dates. |
| Save External Link Values | Saves copies of values contained in a linked external document along with the dependent worksheet. |
| Alternative Expression Evaluation | Enables Excel to use Lotus 1-2-3 files without changes. Evaluates text strings to 0, Boolean expressions to 0, and database criteria according to the rules in 1-2-3. |
| Alternative Formula Entry | Converts formulas entered with Lotus 1-2-3 syntax into Microsoft Excel syntax. |

5. Choose the Calc Now button (F9) to force calculation in all open worksheets and charts or in selected formulas.

6. Choose the Calc Document button to force a calculation in the active document.

7. Press **Enter** or click **OK**.

# Options Color Palette

## *Purpose*

Customizes colors and copies color palettes between open documents.

### To change a color

1. Press **Alt**, **O**, **E** or click the **O**ptions menu and select Color Pal**e**tte.

2. Select a color in the palette and choose the **E**dit command.

3. Select another color from the color box. Increase or decrease **H**ue, **S**at (saturation), **L**um (luminosity), and **R**ed, **G**reen, and **B**lue color tones. With the keyboard, type another number in the corresponding text boxes. With the mouse, control the settings with the up and down triangular icons.

4. When the sample rectangle displays the color you want, press **Enter** or click **OK**.

### To copy a color palette

1. Press **Alt**+**C** or click the **C**opy Colors From drop-down box to see all open documents.

2. Select the document from which you want to copy the color palette.

3. Press **Enter** or click **OK**.

### To reset the color palette

To reset the color palette to its original 16 colors, select the Default button in the Color palette dialog box.

## Options Display

### Purpose

Controls the display of cells and objects. Enables you to turn on or off gridlines and column and row headings.

## *To set display options*

1. Press **Alt**, **O**, **D** or click the **O**ptions menu and select **D**isplay.

2. Turn on Fo**r**mulas to display formulas in cells; turn off Fo**r**mulas to display the resulting values. The default setting is off.

3. Turn on Gridlines to display lines along row and column boundaries. The default setting is on.

4. Turn on Row & Column H**e**adings to display letters across the top of the columns and numbers down the left side of the rows. The default setting is on.

5. Turn on **Z**ero Values to display a 0 in cells with zero values; turn off **Z**ero Values to display blank cells. The default setting is on.

6. Turn on **O**utline Symbols to display symbols used in outlining. The default setting is on.

7. Turn on Automatic Page **B**reaks to display page breaks set by Excel. The default setting is off.

8. Turn on Show **A**ll to display all graphic objects created using Toolbar options. Show **A**ll is the default option.

9. Turn on **S**how Placeholders to display selected pictures and embedded charts as gray rectangles. Other graphic objects, buttons, and text boxes created with Toolbar options are displayed normally.

10. Turn on Hi**d**e All to hide all graphic objects created with the Toolbar options.

11. If your system supports color, you can select a Gridline and Heading **C**olor from the drop-down list. The default setting is Automatic.

12. Press **Enter** or click **OK**.

## Options Group Edit

### Purpose

Enables editing of designated worksheets and macro sheets as a group.

### To group sheets

1. Press **Alt**, **O**, **G** or click the **O**ptions menu and select **G**roup Edit.

2. Select the worksheet and macro sheets to be included in the group. Select contiguous sheets by pressing **Shift** and clicking the sheets. Select discontiguous sheets by pressing **Ctrl** and clicking the sheets.

3. Press **Enter** or click **OK**.

### To ungroup or regroup sheets

1. Press **Alt**, **O**, **G** or click the **O**ptions menu and select **G**roup Edit.

2. To ungroup, simply click a sheet to remove the group. To regroup, deselect a sheet by pressing **Ctrl** and clicking the sheet you want to remove. Add a sheet by pressing **Ctrl** and clicking a sheet.

3. Press **Enter** or click **OK**.

### Note

You can display all the sheets in a group by choosing **W**indow **A**rrange and selecting the Windows of **A**ctive Document box.

# Options Protect (Unprotect) Document

## *Purpose*

Sets (or removes) protection for a document's cells. Sets (or removes) password protection.

## *To protect a document*

1. Press **Alt**, **O**, **P** or click the **O**ptions menu and select **P**rotect Document.

2. Select **C**ells to protect or unprotect the cell as specified by the Forma**t** Cell Protect**i**on dialog box.

3. Select **W**indows to protect or unprotect the document window screen position, size, and other characteristics.

4. Select **O**bjects to protect or unprotect objects specified with the Forma**t** Object Protect**i**on command.

5. To protect your protection settings, select **P**assword and enter any combination of letters, spaces, numbers, or symbols. Excel will prompt you to verify your password.

   You cannot change or unprotect the document unless you remember the password. Passwords are case-sensitive.

6. Press **Enter** or click **OK**.

   If you created a password, reenter your password when prompted, and then press **Enter** or click **OK**.

## *To unprotect a document*

1. Press **Alt**, **O**, **P** or click the **O**ptions menu and select Un**p**rotect Document.

2. If the document is not password-protected, you can now alter the document.

If the document is password-protected, Excel requests a password. Type the appropriate password, and then press **Enter** or click **OK**.

# Options Set (Remove) Page Break

### *Purpose*

Inserts (or deletes) a manual page break.

### *To set a page break*

1. Select the cell to the right and below where you want to insert a page break.

2. Press **Alt, O, B** or click the **O**ptions menu and select Set Page **B**reak.

   Dashed lines appear above and to the left of the active cell.

### *To remove a page break*

1. Position the cell pointer directly below or to the right of the page break you want to remove. (The **O**ptions Remove Page **B**reak command appears only when the cell pointer is in this position.)

2. Press **Alt, O, B** or click the **O**ptions menu and select Remove Page **B**reak.

   This command works on manual page breaks only. You cannot remove automatic page breaks.

# Options Set (Remove) Print Area

### Purpose

Specifies the area of the worksheet to be printed, or deletes the specification of the print area.

### To set the print area

1. Select the worksheet area you want to print.

2. Press **Alt**, **O**, **A** or click the **O**ptions menu and select Set Print **A**rea.

   Dashed lines outline the print area, and Excel internally names the section *Print_Area*.

3. Repeat steps 1 and 2 to define a new print area.

### To remove the print area

1. Press **Ctrl+Shift+space bar** to select the entire worksheet. You also can click in the upper left corner of the worksheet in the cell where the row and column headings intersect.

2. Press **Alt**, **O**, **A** or click the **O**ptions menu and select Remove Print **A**rea. **O**ptions Remove Print **A**rea appears only when the entire worksheet is selected.

# Options Set (Remove) Print Titles

### Purpose

Specifies (or deletes) title text to be printed on every page of a worksheet.

**CAUTION:** Do not include the titles when you set the print area because the titles will print twice.

### To set print titles

1. Enter the title text in the worksheet you want to print. If the text is in adjoining rows or columns, you can include text from anywhere in the worksheet.

2. Select the entire row(s) or column(s) containing the title text.

   With the mouse, select entire rows or columns by clicking their headings.

3. Press **Alt, O, T** or click the **O**ptions menu and select Set Print **T**itles.

4. The Set Print Titles dialog box appears. The Titles for **C**olumns or the Titles for **R**ows box will contain entries if you performed step 2. If you did not select a row(s) or a column(s), you can type in the dimensions of the titles range at this point. If you want to change what appears in the Titles for **C**olumns or the Titles for **R**ows box, edit the dimensions of the titles range.

5. Press **Enter** or click **OK**.

   Excel internally names the section *Print_Titles*. Text in a title cell prints near the top or to the left of every page that contains a worksheet cell in the same column or row.

### To remove print titles

1. Press **Ctrl+Shift+space bar** to select the entire worksheet. You also can click in the upper left corner of the worksheet in the cell where the row and column headings intersect.

2. Press **Alt**, **O**, **T** or click the **O**ptions menu and select Remove Print **T**itles. **O**ptions Remove Print **T**itles appears only when the entire worksheet is selected.

# Options Spelling

### Purpose

Checks the spelling of a selection, a worksheet, or a macro sheet.

### To check spelling

1. Select specific cells to check. If you do not select a range of cells, Excel checks the entire worksheet.

   The spelling check begins at the active cell and checks forward. When the spelling check reaches the end of the document, it asks whether to continue checking at beginning of the worksheet. To check the entire worksheet in one step, make A1 the active cell.

2. Press **Alt**, **O**, **S** or click the **O**ptions menu and select **S**pelling.

3. Choose the appropriate options for the mis-spelled word.

   Change **T**o/Suggestions: The identified word will be replaced by the word in the Change **T**o box when **C**hange is chosen. You can leave the default suggestion, select another word in the suggestion list, or type in a word.

   Add **W**ords To: Adds the identified word to the dictionary in the Add **W**ords To: box. By default, CUSTOM.DIC is the dictionary in the Add **W**ords To box.

Ignore: Leaves the selected word unchanged.

Ignore All: Leaves the selected word unchanged throughout the selection, worksheet, or macro sheet.

Change: Changes the selected word to the word in the Change To: box.

Change All: Changes the selected word to the word in the Change To box throughout the selection, worksheet, or macro sheet.

Add: Adds the selected word to the dictionary in the Add Words To box.

Cancel/Close: Closes the dialog box. Cancel changes to Close if you add a word to a dictionary or you change a misspelled word.

Suggest: Displays a list of proposed suggestions in the Suggestions list box for a word typed into the Change To box.

Ignore Words in UPPERCASE: Causes Spell check to ignore words that contain only capital letters.

Always Suggest: Causes a list of suggested words to display in the Suggestions box for every misspelled word.

4. Press Enter or click OK. To stop the spell check before it is finished, press Esc or click Cancel.

## Options Toolbars

### *Purpose*

Enables you to add, create, edit, display, hide, and customize Toolbars.

### *To display, customize, or create a Toolbar*

1. Press **Alt, O, O** or click the **O**ptions menu and select **T**oolbars.

2. Select the Toolbar you want to change from the Toolbars listed under Show Toolbars.

3. The name of the selected Toolbar displays in the Toolbar **N**ame box. If you are creating a new Toolbar, type the name of the Toolbar in the Toolbar **N**ame box.

4. Choose **S**how to display on-screen the Toolbar in the Toolbar **N**ame box.

   If the Toolbar is already displayed, **S**how becomes **H**ide. If you are creating a new Toolbar, the option is **A**dd. Choose **A**dd to create the new Toolbar.

   A Toolbar with no tools appears on-screen.

5. Choose **H**ide to remove the Toolbar in the Toolbar **N**ame box from the screen.

6. Choose **C**ustomize to add, remove, or change tools on a Toolbar. A dialog box appears with the following elements:

   **C**ategories: Lists all of the tool categories. Each category contains tools specific to that category.

   Tools: Shows the tools that are in the selected category.

   Tool Description: Describes the selected tool.

   **R**eset: Returns the selected Toolbar to the original, or built-in, tool set. Reset changes to **D**elete for a custom Toolbar, and deletes the selected custom Toolbar.

   Close: Closes the dialog box.

   To add a tool to a Toolbar, drag the tool to a Toolbar on-screen and release it on the Toolbar.

To remove a tool from a Toolbar, drag the tool off the Toolbar and release it.

# Options Workspace

### Purpose

Determines decimal and workspace settings that apply to all documents and the surrounding workspace.

### To set the number of decimal places

1. Press **Alt**, **O**, **W** or click the **O**ptions menu and select **W**orkspace.

2. Select Fi**x**ed Decimal and enter the number of decimal places you want in the Places text box. The default for Fi**x**ed Decimal is off. The default for **P**laces is two decimal places. This command does not affect numbers in which you manually insert a decimal point.

3. Select R**1**C1 to display headings and cell references in Row-Column format rather than in Excel's default A1 format. The default setting is off.

4. Select **S**tatus Bar to turn on the status display at the bottom of the screen. The default setting is on.

5. Select Info **W**indow to display the Info window. The default setting is off.

6. Select S**c**roll Bars to turn on the scroll bar display. The default setting is on.

7. Select Fo**r**mula Bar to turn on the display/ editing area at the top of documents. The default setting is on.

8. Select Note Indicator to display a small dot in the top right corner of cells with notes attached. The default setting is on.

9. Change the Alternate Menu or Help key, which duplicates the Alt key's action of selecting the menu bar. Select whether Microsoft Excel Menus or Lotus 1-2-3 Help displays when you press the slash (/) key. The default setting is Microsoft Excel Menus.

10. Select Alternate Navigation Keys to provide a different set of keystrokes for spreadsheet navigation. The default setting is off.

11. Select Ignore Remote Requests to ignore or respond to other Windows applications. The default setting is off.

12. Select Move Selection after Enter to move the active cell down one row after data is entered in a cell. The default setting is off.

13. Select Cell Drag and Drop to be able to move the cells contents by simply dragging the Drag and Drop cell outline to another location. The default is on.

14. Press Enter or click OK.

## Window Activate Window

### Purpose

Lists open documents and enables you to activate a window.

### To activate a window

1. Press Alt, W or click the Window menu to display up to nine open windows.

2. Activate a particular window by typing the number to its left, by clicking the document name, or by pressing **Ctrl+F6**. Only one name appears on the list if you have only one document open.

## Window Arrange

### *Purpose*

Rearranges all on-screen windows to take maximum advantage of available space.

### *To arrange active windows*

1. Press **Alt**, **W**, **A** or click the **W**indows menu and select **A**rrange.

2. The Arrange box provides four ways to arrange the active windows:

   Tiled: Arranges open windows in small sizes so each window fits on-screen. Tiled is the default.

   Horizontal: Arranges windows stacked on top of one another.

   Vertical: Arranges windows from left to right so that each can be seen on-screen.

   None: Enables you to change synchronization without arranging the windows.

3. If Windows of Active Document is selected, only the windows of the active document are arranged. This choice also enables a change to the synchronization of the windows.

   Sync Horizontal: Synchronizes horizontal scrolling in all windows of the active document.

Sync Vertical: Synchronizes vertical scrolling in all windows of the active document.

Both or only one of the Synchronization
choices can be selected.

4. Press **Enter** or click **OK**.

# Window Arrange Icons

## *Purpose*

Arranges all minimized windows. The icons are
arranged at the bottom of the Excel Workspace. This
choice is only available when a minimized window is
active.

## *To arrange active minimized windows*

Press **Alt**, **W**, **A** or click the Windows menu and
select Arrange Icons.

# Window Freeze (Unfreeze) Panes

## *Purpose*

Stops the scrolling of the top and left panes of a
divided worksheet created with the Window Split
command, or reverses the action of the Window
Freeze Panes command, enabling scrolling in all
window panes.

## *To freeze or unfreeze panes*

Press **Alt**, **W**, **F** or click the Windows menu and
select Freeze (or Unfreeze) Panes.

### Notes

Window Freeze Panes keeps row or column titles
stationary. If you do not first create a pane with the
Window Split command, Window Freeze creates
four quadrants on the current window.

See also *Window Split*.

## Window Hide (Unhide)

### Purpose

Makes the active window invisible (the document
remains open and can be unhidden), or lists all
hidden windows and displays the window you
select.

### To hide the active window

Press Alt, W, H or click the Window menu and
select Hide.

### To unhide a window

1. Press Alt, W, U or click the Window menu and
   select Unhide. (If all windows are hidden, this
   command appears on the File menu.)

2. Select the window you want to display and
   press Enter or click OK.

   For windows protected with the Options
   Protect Document command and a password,
   Excel asks for the password before unhiding
   the window.

# Window More Windows

## *Purpose*

Lists the names of all windows and activates the window you select. This command appears only when more than nine windows are open.

## *To list window names*

1. Press **Alt**, **W**, **M** or click the **W**indow menu and select **M**ore Windows.

2. Scroll through the list of open windows and select the one you want to activate.

3. Press **Enter** or click **OK**.

# Window New Window

## *Purpose*

Creates an additional window for the active document.

## *To create a new window*

1. Press **Alt**, **W**, **N** or click the **W**indow menu and select **N**ew Window.

2. To create additional windows, repeat this procedure.

3. To activate a window, click a visible window; select a window from the **W**indow menu; or press **Ctrl+F6** repeatedly.

4. For synchronized scrolling, click the **W**indow menu and select **A**rrange. Then choose **S**ync Horizontal and/or S**y**nc Vertical under Windows of **A**ctive Document.

## Window Split

### *Purpose*

Creates a split in the window of two or four panes, which enables you to scroll multiple panes. The split can also be used to freeze a portion of the window on-screen using the **W**indow **F**reeze Panes command.

### *To split a window*

1. Press **Alt**, **W**, **S** or click the **W**indow menu and select **S**plit.

2. Move the split bars into position to fit your needs. You can move the vertical pane divider left or right. You can move the horizontal pane divider up or down.

   If you need to freeze the part of the window either above the horizontal pane divider or to the left of the vertical pane divider, choose **W**indow **F**reeze Panes.

### *To remove a split in a window*

Press **Alt**, **W**, **S** or click the **W**indow menu and select Remove **S**plit to remove the split. You can also remove a split by simply double-clicking it.

# Window Zoom

## *Purpose*

Displays a worksheet at different magnifications.

## *To magnify a worksheet or a portion of a worksheet*

1.  Activate the sheet you want to magnify.

2.  Press **Alt**, **W**, **Z** or click **W**indow and select **Z**oom.

3.  There are five preset magnifications:

    20**0**: Enables you to view the worksheet in detail.

    1**00**: The default; normal magnification.

    **7**5: Enables you to view more of the spread-sheet.

    **5**0: Enables you to view double the normal spreadsheet area.

    **2**5: Enables you to get a good overview of the worksheet. This view can be difficult to work in.

4.  Choose **F**it Selection to magnify the window so that only the selected cells display. Before choosing this option, you must select cells on the worksheet.

5.  The **C**ustom choice enables you to tailor the magnification to a more specific view. You can select a zoom factor between 10 and 400.

6.  Press **Enter** or click **OK**.

# INDEX